An Outline of

OLD TESTAMENT
HISTORY

An Outline of

OLD TESTAMENT HISTORY

By
CHARLES F. PFEIFFER

MOODY PRESS
CHICAGO

IBSN: 0-8024-6265-0
Printed in the United States of America

CONTENTS

List of Maps

CHAPTER 1

INTRODUCTION

IN THE WIDEST SENSE, Old Testament history covers the period from the creation of the world to the return of Israel from Babylonian exile. Its prime source materials are in the Old Testament itself. Historical books are found in all three sections of the Hebrew canon—the law, prophets and writings. Biblical books of poetry and prophecy contain allusions to historical events, and their witness must be added to that of the historical books in the attempt to get a complete picture of the history recorded in Scripture.

The Scope of Old Testament History. Most of Old Testament history centers around the people or nation of Israel. The first eleven chapters of Genesis deal with mankind as a whole, from creation to the dispersion of the sons of Noah. These chapters form an introduction to the call of Abraham and the beginnings of Israel as a separate people. The rest of the Old Testament continues the history of Abraham's descendants to the time of their return from Babylonian captivity during the time when the Persians ruled the Near East.

The canonical books of the Old Testament do not record the

7

history of the Jews between the time of Malachi and the beginnings of New Testament history. Daniel makes some prophetic allusions to this period. The writings of Flavius Josephus, the Jewish historian, and the apocryphal book of I Maccabees provide detailed information. Other apocryphal literature and the writers of the Hellenistic age add to our knowledge of the Judaism of the period before the birth of Christ.

The Sources of Old Testament History. The one indispensable tool for a knowledge of Bible history is the Bible itself. Although its earliest writings do not antedate 1500 B.C., it gives us a careful, accurate record of the history it records. The theologian speaks of the Bible as an inspired book—God's Word to man. The historian regards it as an accurate record of God's dealings with man.

The age of modern archaeological discovery has provided the Bible student with a wealth of written material from Palestine and adjacent lands. Some of this material is contemporary with the Biblical records. We may read Sennacherib's own account of his siege of Jerusalem and Cyrus' record of his policy of returning captive peoples to their ancestral homes. While we cannot expect to find parallels to every episode of Biblical history, the number of such parallels is amazing. It would be hard to exaggerate the importance of the literature of the ancient Near East as an aid to the understanding of the Bible. Even a hasty examination of a volume such as Pritchard's *Ancient Near Eastern Texts Relating to the Old Testament* will indicate the wealth of factual material which must be assimilated and applied by the careful student of Bible history.

Sumerian records date back to about 3000 B.C. Accounts of creation and the flood must be compared with the Biblical records. The Sumerian King List records the names of kings who reigned "before the flood." Interesting comparisons and contrasts can be drawn between these and the Biblical antediluvians. The flood account of the Sumerians and their Babylonian successors has so many points in common with the Biblical record that a common origin for the two accounts is indisputable.

Cuneiform literature provides an essential backdrop for the patriarchal records. Tablets discovered at Nuzu, near Kirkuk, and Mari on the Euphrates, illustrate customs previously known only from the Genesis record. The migrations of Abraham and his descendants, the sojourn in Egypt, the Exodus and the subsequent conquest of Canaan can now be seen against the background of the laws and customs of Sumerians, Babylonians, Mittanians (in whose territory Haran was located), Hurrians (Biblical Horites), Hittites and Egyptians.

From the time of the United Kingdom to the close of Old Testament history the extra-Biblical sources become even more numerous. Kings of Israel and Judah are mentioned by name on the monuments of Assyrians, Babylonians and Persians. Moabites commemorate victories over Israelites. Letters from Lachish, written on broken pieces of pottery (*ostraca*) describe the last phases of Nebuchadnezzar's conquest of Judah.

The primary sources of Old Testament history are:

The Bible—both historical books and historical allusions in other books.

Cuneiform literature—the clay tablets of the ancient Sumerians, Assyrians, Babylonians, Hittites, Canaanites and their neighbors. This literature helps us to understand the environment in which the Biblical events took place. In the broadest sense this is true of legal contracts, letters, law codes, religious and mythological texts as well as the historical annals of these nations.

Hieroglyphic literature—Egypt, like the cuneiform world, produced a varied body of literature which dates back to 3000 B.C. The decipherment of Hittite hieroglyphs promises to be another fruitful source of information.

Greek and Roman historians—For centuries our knowledge of the ancient world was limited to the Bible and the classical historians of Greece and Rome. Cuneiform and hieroglyphic literature is much more valuable for the early periods of Bible history, but the classical writers should not be overlooked. Herodotus is an excellent source of information for the world of the fifth century before Christ. His accuracy diminishes, however, the farther his writings are removed from his own generation.

Other ancient historians—Fragments have reached us from the Egyptian historian Manetho (c. 300 B.C.), who divided the political history of Egypt into thirty-one dynasties. This division of Egyptian history is still used, largely as a matter of convenience. Philo of Byblos incorporates writings which he ascribes to the ancient Phoenician historian Sanchuniathon.

Ancient Jewish literature—The literature of the apocrypha and pseudepigrapha is helpful in understanding the development of Jewish life in the Hellenistic-Roman age. The Dead Sea Scrolls provide further source material for this enigmatic period. The writings of Josephus make no substantial contribution to Biblical history before the Persian period.

Semitic inscriptions—Semitic inscriptions are few in number compared with the large quantities of cuneiform and hieroglyphic inscriptions. They help us to understand something of the language as well as the history of Israel, however. In this category are the Gezer Calendar, listing the months in the order of agricultural activity (10th century B.C.), the Moabite Stone (c. 830 B.C.) and the Siloam Inscription, dating from the time of Hezekiah.

The Biblical Approach to History. The great desideratum of modern scientific methodology is objectivity. Scholars seek to evaluate all of the evidence in a given matter and then arrive at conclusions which are based on that evidence alone. Presuppositions are considered incompatible with an objective viewpoint.

It is recognized, however, that complete objectivity is never actually realized. We need not go beyond the study of history for examples. A historian may write from the viewpoint that men make history, as did Carlyle. Others may write from the viewpoint that history produces the man. Did Martin Luther cause the Protestant Reformation, or did the forces of fifteenth-century German religious, political and social life produce a Luther? To some historians, particularly those with strong Marxist tendencies, economics is the cause not only of war, but of almost all social phenomena. To Freud, human behavior is largely motivated by sex. A Darwin is sure that an evolutionary philosophy will account for social as well as physical change. A Toynbee looks upon history as a series of cycles.

It is not surprising that such varied explanations of the phenomena of history should arise. The important thing to note, however, is that each historian can marshal an imposing array of facts to prove his view of history. Each feels that he is being thoroughly objective.

It should not be surprising that the Bible contains a philosophy of history. To the Bible writers God is both the first Cause and the instrumental Agent in history. Without Him there could be no history. Bible history is written to glorify God. The deeds of wicked men are recorded that the reader might be forewarned. The deeds of the righteous are recorded that the godly might emulate them.

The apostle John stated that he chose certain episodes from the life of Christ for inclusion in his Gospel that the reader might "believe that Jesus is the Christ, the Son of God." He makes it clear that his is not a complete biography of Jesus. From the wealth of available material, John chose that material which was particularly suited to his purpose. The same can be said of other historical books in the Bible. The Old Testament writers did not write a history of the Near East or of Israel. They wanted their readers to know the wisdom, power, holiness and love of the God of Israel. We might wish to know much that is unrecorded. They did not write to answer our intellectual curiosity, however. They wrote that which would produce an attitude of faith and obedience.

The Natural and the Supernatural. The historian is interested in cause and effect. He observes the actions of men and nations and notes their consequences. He notes that Zedekiah relied on Egyptian aid and refused to pay his tribute to Nebuchadnezzar with the result that the Neo-Babylonian armies besieged, captured and destroyed Jerusalem, taking its leading citizens into exile.

The theologian will approach the same data but may use different terminology. He will note that the history of Judah was one of rebellion against God. Idolatry grew rampant after the short-lived revival under King Josiah. As a punishment for sin, Judah was conquered and its people exiled.

The historical and the theological approaches to history are contradictory only if God is removed from the historical processes. The Bible writers saw no contradiction whatever. All of the processes of history are subject to His control, and he usually works through them.

The death of Christ is attributed both to the wickedness of men and the sovereign, gracious purposes of God: "Him, being delivered by the determinate counsel and foreknowledge of God, ye have taken, and by wicked hands have crucified and slain" (Acts 2:23). In making himself known to the brethren who had sold him into Egyptian slavery, Joseph said, "Now, therefore be not grieved, nor angry with yourselves, that ye sold me hither: for God did send me before you to preserve life" (Gen. 45:5). Scripture emphasizes both the responsibility of man for his acts and the sovereignty of God in the historical processes.

Every reader of the Bible is conscious of the large place which the supernatural plays in sacred history. The miraculous crossing of the Red Sea, the manna in the wilderness, the crossing of the Jordan, the fall of Jericho, the fire which consumed Elijah's sacrifice, the destruction of the armies of Sennacherib and numerous other examples could be cited. Yet it should be remembered that the miracle is the exception, not the rule. The God of the Bible is pictured as omnipotent. He is the Author of nature, just as He is the Author of supernatural events.

During the wilderness wanderings Israel was unable to plant seed and await harvests. The "waste howling wilderness" could not provide sustenance of itself for the people in their wanderings. God saw fit to preserve His people by means of a miracle repeated six times a week for forty years. Joshua 4 records the crossing of the Jordan preparatory to the conquest of Canaan. Joshua 5 states that the miracle of the manna ceased, "neither had the children of Israel manna any more; but they did eat of the fruit of the land of Canaan that year" (5:12).

Bible history describes the activity of God in human affairs, particularly as they affect the people who bear His name. Normally He acts through the processes which we call nature. Nature has been defined as "the habits of God." Men sense no violation of their freedom as they accomplish God's purposes. Nebuchadnezzar was not aware of the fact that he was a divine agent for the chastisement of rebellious Israel. Judas Iscariot was unaware of the fact that his act of treason was helping to fulfill the sovereign purposes of God.

The recognition that all history, whether natural or supernatural in our terminology, is subject to God and issues in the accomplishment of His purposes enables us to give due attention to the secondary cause and effect relationships. They possess reality, under God. Recognizing God as the Sovereign of history does not remove the necessity for the study of history. It gives it a new and fuller meaning than it could have otherwise.

CHAPTER 2

THE EARLIEST AGES

Creation. Biblical history begins with a simple, yet majestic statement concerning God. He is the Creator of all that exists, for the terms "heaven and earth" are the ancient Hebrew words which convey the thought of "the universe." The fact of creation forms a fitting introduction to Biblical history. The infinite God is contrasted with His finite creation. Creation itself implies dependence. Man owes his very being to his Creator.

The interpretation of the details of the creation record is not easy. The idea that the world was created in six days of twenty-four hours each about six thousand years ago (4004 B.C.— Ussher's Chronology) was long held to be the teaching of Scripture. Our knowledge of geology and other sciences, including archaeology, make it impossible for any informed individual to hold that viewpoint today. Some do hold to six literal days of creation in remote antiquities.

No one view concerning the Biblical account of creation has

14

gained universal assent. Current views among evangelical Christians include:

1. *The "Gap" Hypothesis.* According to this view the initial creation of Genesis 1:1 is considered complete and perfect. A catastrophe, involving the fall of the angels, is posited between 1:1 and 1:2, after which the six days of "re-creation" take place. The expression "the earth was without form, and void" is rendered "the earth became without form and void" by those who see here a reference to a cataclysmic judgment. Since there is no time reference between the creation of 1:1 and the re-creation during the six "days," adherents of this view account for the geological ages by placing them within the "gap" between 1:1 and 1:2. Some adherents of the Gap Hypothesis believe in a pre-Adamic race which populated the earth before the judgment of 1:2 (cf. G. H. Pember, *Earth's Earliest Ages*). The dubious nature of the evidence for the Gap Hypothesis is discussed in Oswald T. Allis, *God Spake by Moses,* Appendix 1.

2. *The Concordance Theory.* Many scholars equate the six "days" of creation with as many geological ages. Although ingenious lists are drawn up to indicate the parallelism between the "days" of Genesis and geology, most scholars consider them forced. Geological ages are not capable of rigid division, and the creation of the stars on the fourth day is particularly hard to place in any such system.

3. *Days of Dramatic Vision.* This theory suggests that Adam (or Moses) received from God a series of revelations concerning the creative activity. The "days" are not considered chronological in the order of creation but in the order of revelation. This removes certain of the problems indicated in the other viewpoints, but it must be admitted that this view is devoid of any positive scriptural evidence. It is true, of course, that man was not a witness to the creative events, and that any valid knowledge would come through revelation. The "Dramatic Vision" view differs from the others largely in its abandonment of chronological significance for the "six days." The division of the "days" into two groups of three each is considered a device of revelation. Thus the creation of light (the first day)

and the creation of the luminaries (the fourth day) have a literary relationship.

Although the exact date and the details of creation are not known to us, the purpose of the creation account is clear. God brought the world into being without the use of pre-existent material. All things—including such objects of heathen worship as the sun, moon and stars—were made by Him. The crown of creation was man, made in the "image of God" and endowed with the capacity of fellowship with his Maker.

The First Man. Created with the capacity for self-determination, Adam and his wife, Eve, were placed in the beautiful Garden of Eden. The environment was a perfect one, designed of God for man's good. The prohibition which served as a test must not be thought of as inconsistent with God's goodness. God had been most generous with man, and the prohibition involved nothing essential to man's life or happiness.

Two of the rivers bounding man's first home are known to us. The Tigris and the Euphrates water the region known to historians as Mesopotamia ("the land between the rivers"). The Hiddekel, described as one of the boundaries of Eden, is known to be the Tigris. The Pishon and the Gihon cannot be identified, with the result that the location of Eden is a matter of conjecture. Some location in the Tigris-Euphrates Valley is obviously meant, but more than that we cannot say.

The Fall. Biblical history works with the presupposition that man is a sinner. Although the creation account describes all of creation as "very good," history is replete with natural and moral catastrophe—murder, warfare, theft, flood, pestilence, sickness and death. Some of these are directly related to sin, and others do not seem to have any moral factor. Yet the Bible traces all ill, natural as well as moral, to an act of rebellion against God early in human history.

Scripture presents our first parents, dwelling in a perfect environment, as subjected to a test in the form of forbidden fruit. Through the cunning of the serpent, Satan urged Eve to transgress the commandment of God by doing that which had been forbidden. She looked upon the forbidden fruit and found it pleasant. She desired the wisdom which the tempter stated would result from eating it. Eve ate of the fruit and gave some of it to her husband, who also ate.

Man's sense of shame which found expression in his act of hiding from God was an immediate consequence of his disobedience. Sorrow in childbearing and subjection to her husband were defined as the lot of the woman. Difficult toil on ground that had itself been cursed was to be the labor of man. The serpent was degraded, but hope was held out to fallen man in that one day the "seed of the woman" would bruise the head of the "serpent" although, in so doing, his "heel" would be bruised (Gen. 3:15).

The garden, the place of man's primitive bliss, was not a suitable home for fallen man. Adam and Eve were expelled from their paradise and began life under circumstances which are essentially similar to ours. The "curse" is still with us and will remain here until the second coming of Christ, at which time creation itself shall be delivered from its bondage (Rom. 8:21-23).

Is the account of the fall to be taken as literal history, or does it present truth in poetic form? The story of the "talking serpent" is regarded by some Bible students as a kind of parable used to describe man's sinful rebellion against God. Albertus Pieters in his *Notes on Genesis* insists on the historicity of the fall and its consequences, but suggests that the form in which the account of the fall is given may not accord with our sense of history. The ancient view that the sin of our first parents was concupiscence suggests a kind of allegorical view of the story of the fall. This view, incidentally, is an erroneous one, since procreation was a command of God (Gen. 1:28), and asceticism was not the Old Testament ideal.

As in the case of the creation accounts, so in the matter of the fall, the accounts themselves have been interpreted in various ways, but the fact is clear and basic to Biblical studies. The Bible teaches us that our first parents sinned against God, will-

fully and after having been adequately warned. The results of
this sin are seen in the world in which we live, and in our own
lives as sinful creatures. The New England Primer summarized
it in the words:

> *In Adam's fall*
> *We sinnéd all.*

Cain and Abel (Gen. 4:1-16). Adam and Eve were the
parents of a large family (Gen. 4:17; 5:4), although only three
sons are mentioned in Scripture. Two of these, Cain and Abel,
are described as having offered sacrifices to God. Abel, a shep-
herd, offered of the firstlings of his flock, but Cain, a farmer,
offered of the fruit of the ground a sacrifice to the Lord. Abel's
offering, presented "by faith" (Heb. 11:4), was acceptable to
God, whereas Cain's was evidently offered in a perfunctory manner, devoid of any spiritual content. Jealous of Abel, whose
sacrifice was acceptable to God, Cain spurned the divine warning and murdered his brother. Disclaiming any responsibilitv
as his brother's keeper, Cain was banished to the land of Nod
(i.e., "wandering") to the east of Eden.

Cultural Beginnings (Gen. 4:17-24). Ancient polytheistic
religions considered the gods as inventors of the arts and crafts.
The Egyptian Ptah, the Greek Hephaestus and the Germanic
Vulcan were artisans worshiped by mortals. Israelite monothe-
ism could not tolerate such idolatry. Culture is presented in the
Bible as beginning with the line of Cain who, himself, built a
city. The building of a city early served as a protective device.
A community of individuals with simple fortifications would be
able to defend itself against marauders who might prey on
isolated farmers or herdsmen.

In the line of Cain we read of Jabel, the forerunner of tent
dwellers and cattle breeders. The children of Jubal are credited
with the invention of music. Tubal-cain was the first metal-
lurgist.

Cultural progress brought with it the temptation to empha-
size material rather than spiritual realities. Lamech married

two wives, the first recorded polygamy. He boasted, in a vengeful spirit, that he would kill the man who had inflicted a wound on him: "I kill a man for wounding me, a youth for bruising me."

The Sethites (Gen. 4:25—5:32). In the line of Seth, the family of Adam makes a new beginning. The Cain line grew more and more degenerate. In the days of Enos, Seth's son, however, we read that "men began to call on the name of the LORD." The line of Seth includes individuals with the longest life-span in the Bible. Methuselah lived 969 years, although his father Enoch had a life-span of only 365 years. This Enoch, however, goes down as one of the most godly men of Scripture. He was "translated that he should not see death" after a life in which he "walked with God" (cf. Heb. 11:5).

The Problem of Longevity. The exceptionally long lifespans of the antediluvians have challenged scholarly thought over the years. Attempts at solving the problem by means of "lunar years" (i.e., months) are not convincing as they provide greater problems. Enoch, according to the "lunar year" viewpoint, was but five and one-half years old at the birth of Methuselah! Many nations have traditions of longevity for their earliest patriarchs. Early Sumerian rulers are reputed to have reigned from 21,600 to 72,000 years each. Egypt, Persia and India have comparable traditions. There appears to be an almost universal tradition of exceptional longevity for individuals living in the earliest ages of history.

CHAPTER 3

THE FLOOD

AFTER THE DEVELOPMENT of Cainite culture and the break-down of moral distinctions preserved by the Sethite line, Scripture declares that a flood of enormous proportions destroyed the race of the antediluvians with the exception of Noah and his family.

Causes of the Flood (Gen. 6:1-4). The Biblical flood, unlike its counterparts in the ancient Near Eastern literature, had a moral basis. Genesis declares that "the sons of God" married "the daughters of men." An ancient interpretation of this cryptic statement, contained in the Book of Enoch, declares that angels ("sons of God") married human women ("daughters of men") in violation of the divine order. In modern times this view has been held both by some who accept it as fact and by others who deem it a remnant of Hebrew mythology preserved by the writer of Genesis.

Another viewpoint, however, sees in the intermarriage a

breaking down of the spiritual distinctions preserved in the lines of Seth and Cain. According to this view the godly line of Seth was corrupted by such marriages with the result that "every imagination of man's heart was only evil continually." In view of the fact that the judgment of the flood is described as falling on "man," and that no hint of angels (beyond the reference to "sons of God") appears in the narrative, many conservative writers dismiss the thought of marrying angels as an erroneous viewpoint.

The Flood Itself. After Noah had prepared his ark and brought into it his family, seven of each of the clean animals and two of each of the unclean animals, the flood began. The rains came down and the "fountains of the deep" were opened for forty days. The land was covered with water for a solar year of 365 days.

The actions of doves and a raven released by Noah signaled the time when the waters had abated and it was safe to leave the ark. Thereupon Noah offered burnt offerings and God made the rainbow to serve as a sign that the earth would not again be destroyed by water.

Evidences of the Flood. Palestinian cities, including Jericho, have a history which goes back to 5000 B.C. with no archaeological evidence of a flood. In Mesopotamia, however, the situation is different. Sir Leonard Woolley found a stratum of river mud or flood silt eight feet thick at Ur. Other deposits, significantly later than those of Ur, have been discovered at Fara and Kish. Nineveh appears to have had a flood about the same time as that which Woolley discovered at Ur. Since considerable variation exists in the level of "flood silt" and the dates of the layers, we cannot affirm that the silt from any one city is that of the Biblical deluge. They rather indicate that extensive floods were common in Mesopotamia.

Parallel Flood Stories. Remarkable parallels to the Biblical flood account appear in the literature of ancient Sumer and Babylon. In the Gilgamesh Epic, the Babylonian Noah, Utnapishtim by name, saved himself and his family along with representatives of the animal creation, by taking refuge in a ship which he had made at the behest of Ea, one of the gods. Like Noah, Utnapishtim sent out birds to reconnoiter and, after the waters receded, he offered sacrifices. The Babylonian flood story does not possess the moral character of the Biblical account, however. The Babylonian gods are arbitrary in their actions, whereas the God of Noah is pictured as righteous in all His deeds. The gods of Utnapishtim are depicted as swarming like flies about the sacrificer, presumably because they have been deprived of their "food" during the flood. Such crass elements are totally missing from the Biblical flood account.

The related flood accounts of the Sumerians and the Babylonians are closest in form and content to that of the Bible. Flood traditions exist, however, in widely scattered areas. Records from Syria, Asia Minor, Iran, Egypt, India and even Australia are sometimes cited.

Extent of the Flood. The records of Genesis (6:6, 7, 17, 18; 7:19, 20) seem to imply that the deluge covered the entire earth and that all men and land animals were destroyed. That God could have performed the necessary miracle to cover the earth with water five and one-half miles above sea level during a forty-day rain (augmented by subterranean waters) must be granted, for with God "all things are possible." We dare not neglect, however, to examine evidence from geology and other sources which may throw light on the means which God used in bringing about the destruction of the antediluvians.

The Biblical flood cannot be equated with the waters of the tertiary period or of the Ice Age. These were both long periods of time, whereas the Bible speaks of a storm lasting only forty days and a flood of a year's duration.

Many Biblical scholars feel that the flood was universal anthropologically, but not geologically, i.e., that it covered the entire land inhabited by man at the period of the flood, but not the whole earth. This view presupposes that man had not migrated to distant parts of the globe until after the flood. It might also imply that animals had not migrated beyond the confines of man's habitation, although an alternative has been suggested: animals from the region where man lived were taken into the ark so that they could be replaced at the end of the flood. If this had not been done it would have been necessary to await migrations from distant regions.

The date of the flood (see below) has some bearing on the question of its extent. No universal flood during historic times (i.e., since the beginning of writing, c. 3000 B.C.) has left evidence which can be scientifically studied. Some scholars interpret earlier geological phenomena as indicative of a universal deluge.

Date of the Flood. Unless we are willing to dismiss the varied flood stories of widely scattered peoples as exaggerations of local catastrophes, we must recognize a flood of great, if not universal, extent early in human history. Sumerian flood traditions are dated back at least to the third millennium B.C. The flood itself was, of course, much earlier. The antediluvians were a dim memory in the minds of the Sumerians at the earliest period of their history.

Neither Biblical nor archaeological evidence provides conclusive evidence for the date of the flood. Both suggest that the flood took place very early in history, before the dispersion of the nations, and that it was of such proportions as to leave an indelible impression on the minds of people in succeeding generations all over the world.

CHAPTER 4

THE NATIONS

THE LAND OF PALESTINE occupies a strategic spot at the eastern end of the Mediterranean Sea. Although Israel maintained a position of separation from her neighbors during important periods of history, she was always aware of their existence and of the threat—military and religious—which they offered.

The Table of Nations (Gen. 10). Relationships between Israel and her neighbors are summarized in the Table of Nations which traces the lineage of peoples of the ancient Near East to the three sons of Noah. It should be noted that individuals and peoples occur in the list. Nimrod is clearly an individual, whereas "the Jebusite, and the Amorite, and the Girgasite" (Gen. 10:16) are peoples. In some instances it is not easy to determine whether individuals or nations are intended.

Japheth. The term Aryan, or Indo-European, is frequently used of the peoples designated as Japhetic in earlier writings. Genesis speaks of seven families or "sons of Japheth" and seven others designated as his grandsons (Gen.10:2-4).

24

Gomer, known to the Greeks as the Kimmerioi, appears to have been a people who inhabited the region north of the Caucasus Mountains. They threatened the Assyrian empire until defeated by Esarhaddon. For a time they overran Asia Minor, but they were driven out by Alyattes of Lydia.

Three sons of Gomer are mentioned in the Table of Nations: Ashkenaz, Riphath and Togarmah. Little is known of these peoples. Jeremiah refers to Ashkenaz as a people dwelling in Armenia (51:27). The Greeks spoke of the Riphaean Mountains as the northern extremity of the world. Ezekiel places Togarmah "in the uttermost parts of the north" (38:6). None of these peoples had important relations with Israel, although Togarmah is said to have traded war horses and mules for the luxury wares of Tyre (Ezek. 27:14).

Magog was identified by Josephus with the Scythians, although modern scholarship does not take the suggestion seriously. The Amarna Tablets from the fourteenth century B.C. Egypt mention a people called Gagaia, which may be related to the kindred word, Gog (cf. Ezek. 38 and 39).

The word Madai is uniformly translated Medes, a people who lived south of the Caspian Sea and became the Median Empire which joined forces with Babylon to bring about the destruction of Nineveh in 612 B.C. Under Cyrus, the Medes were incorporated into the Persian Empire and their separate history came to an end.

Javan, related to the word Ionian, is the usual word rendered Greece in the English Bible. It refers both to the Greeks of the mainland and those who settled in western Asia Minor. In Genesis 10:4 the Ionians appear in four subdivisions: Elishah, Tarshish, Kittim, Rodanim (Dodanim). Elishah seems to refer to the western Greeks of Sicily and southern Italy. Tarshish, meaning "smelting plant" or "refinery," was the name of several localities in the ancient world. The Tarshish of Genesis 10 may refer to Sardinia, or to Tartessus in southern Spain, near Gibraltar. The Kittim (or Chittim) are, strictly speaking, the inhabitants of Cyprus, where Kitium is a principal city. Later the term seems to have been used of islanders in general. It appears in the Dead Sea Scrolls and in Post-Biblical Jewish literature where it refers to the Romans.

Dodanim, the form used in Genesis 10:4, has a parallel form, Rodanim, in I Chronicles 1:7. The letters "D" and "R" are very similar in the Hebrew square script, resulting in the confusion in the two readings. Dodanim might refer to the Danunim people of Cilicia, mentioned in the Phoenician Karatepe inscription, or the Dardanians of Homer's *Iliad,* a name applied to the people of Troy. The term Rodanim would suggest the Isle of Rhodes in the Aegean Sea.

As for Tubal and Meshech, Assyrian texts mention a Tabalu in Asia Minor and a Mushki in eastern Phrygia. In Scripture the two names are generally associated (Ezek. 27:13; 32:26; 38:3; 39:1).

Tiras is probably to be identified with the Tyrsenoi of classical tradition, occupying islands and coast lands of the Aegean. They may be the piratical sea people known as Turusha who invaded Syria and Egypt during the thirteenth century before Christ.

Ham. The Hamitic peoples, whose home was both in Asia and in northern Africa, had early contacts with Israel, usually as enemies. Several sons and grandsons of Ham are mentioned in Genesis, chapter 10. Cush, or Nubia, was the region south of the first cataract of the Nile River. The term is usually rendered "Ethiopia" in our English Bibles, following ancient Greek usage. Five subdivisions of Cush are mentioned: Seba, Havilah, Sabtah, Raamah and Sabtechah. Seba appears to have been located in Africa, probably near Cush. Havilah is located in central Arabia. Sabtah, or Sabata (*Shabwat* in the South Arabic Inscriptions), was the capital of Hadramaut, a district on the southeastern coast of Arabia. Raamah has not been identified, but it is believed to have been located in southwestern Arabia. Two subdivisions of Raamah are mentioned: Sheba, the land of the Yemenite Sabaeans, and Dedan, a people of northwestern Arabia settled along the Red Sea. Sabtechah was probably in southeastern Arabia, but nothing certain is known of it.

Nimrod is named as the founder of an early empire in Babylon. He colonized Assyria (Gen. 10:11) and gained renown as an empire-builder. The cities of Babel, Erech and Accad are among the oldest cities known to man. Thousands of clay tablets from these and other cities of Mesopotamia have made it possible for us to reconstruct much of the history of the Near East—going back to 3000 B.C. The name Accad is used for the Semitic language spoken in this region (Accadian or Akkadian), as the name Sumerian describes the non-Semitic people and language of Southern Mesopotamia.

Mizraim is grammatically a dual form, rendered into English by the word Egypt. The term suggests the historical division of Egypt into two sections: Lower Egypt, comprising the Nile Delta region, and Upper Egypt, comprising the Nile River Valley south of the Delta as far as the First Cataract.

The family of Mizraim (Egypt) has branches including Ludim, Anamim, Lehabim, Naphtuhim, Pathrusim, Casluhim and Caphtorim. The Ludim are North African peoples who served as bowmen in the Egyptian and Tyrian armies (Isa. 66:19; Ezek. 27:10). The Lehabim, or Lubim, are known to us as the Lybians, dwelling on the southern shore of the Mediterranean, west of Egypt. Sheshonk, Biblical Shishak, the Pharaoh who founded the Twenty-second Dynasty of Egypt was a Lybian. He invaded Judah during the reign of Rehoboam (II Chron. 12:2-9). The Caphtorim are generally identified with the inhabitants of Crete, Egyptian *Keftiu*. Caphtor is the home of the Philistines (Amos 9:7) who brought a high degree of culture with them when they occupied southern Palestine. Nothing certain is known of the Anamim, Naphtuhim or Casluhim. The Pathrusim are the people of Pathros, or southern Egypt (Jer 44:15).

Put, or Phut, appears to be related to the Old Persian *Putaya*, a district west of the Nile Delta. Another suggested identification is with Punt, modern Somaliland in East Africa.

Canaan is the familiar Biblical name for the land of the Phoenicians and Canaanites of Syria and Palestine. Since Canaan was closely related to Israel much space is given to a discussion of the Canaanite peoples. The Phoenician city of

Sidon is termed the "firstborn" of Canaan. It is mentioned in the Amarna Tablets (c. 1400 B.C.) and appears to have been the greatest of the Phoenician cities until outstripped by its "daughter" Tyre. The "sons of Heth" are the Hittites who had numerous settlements in Palestine and frequent contacts with Israel (cf. Uriah, Ephron). Hittites had important political and cultural centers in Asia Minor along the Halys River during the second millennium before Christ. They rivaled the Egyptians in power and maintained a "sphere of influence" in northern Canaan, corresponding to that held by Egypt in the south.

Among the "sons" of Canaan are the inhabitants of Syrian cities: Arkites from Arqa, Arvadites from Arvad, and Hamathites from Hamath. Jebusites are Canaanites from Jebus, the city conquered by David and occupied as his capital—Jerusalem.

Shem. The name Shem underlies our word Shemitic, or Semitic, a term usually applied to the Israelites, but actually of much wider significance. Five major branches of Semites are discussed in Genesis 10, with considerable elaboration of the genealogies.

Elam was the province east of the Tigris and north of the Persian Gulf. Elamites were a warlike people who frequently invaded the Tigris-Euphrates Valley and plundered the more highly civilized settlements there. The whole of Persia was frequently termed Elam. It is now known as Iran.

Asshur, or Assyria, became an important empire in northern Mesopotamia, conquering Babylon to the south and the western lands as far as the Mediterranean. In 722 B.C. the Northern Kingdom of Israel fell to the Assyrians, but Judah maintained its independence until after the fall of Nineveh (612 B.C.), Assyria's capital on the Tigris River.

Arphaxad or Arpachshad is the line which includes Eber (whence the name Hebrew) and the family of Abraham. Another branch of the Arphaxad line was that of Joktan, the progenitor of thirteen Arabian tribes which dwelt in the southeastern and southern sections of the Arabian Peninsula.

Lud is representative of the Lydians of Asia Minor whose fabulously wealthy king, Croesus, was defeated by Cyrus the Great.

Aram, or Syria, was a territory north of Israel, inhabited by people known as Aramaeans. The region around Haran was known as Paddan-aram, "the fields of Aram," and Laban, Jacob's uncle, was called an Aramaean. Important Aramaean states arose after the twelfth and eleventh centuries B.C.

THE TABLE OF NATIONS

CHAPTER 5

THE PATRIARCHAL AGE

THE BIBLICAL PATRIARCHS, Abraham, Isaac, Jacob, and Joseph, were men of considerable wealth and prestige. Although they forsook the civilized life of the city and measured their wealth in movable property, they must not be thought of as uncultured individuals. Excavations at Ur, Nuzu, Mari and other ancient sites have helped us to place the Biblical records in their historical context with the result that we can now see the Biblical patriarchs in the light of the culture and customs of the era in which they lived.

Ur of the Chaldees. According to Genesis 11:31, Terah, the father of Abraham, migrated from the territory of Ur to the city of Haran in northwestern Mesopotamia. Although ex-

30

act dates are debatable, this probably took place about 2000 B.C. Excavations at Ur directed by Sir Leonard Woolley from 1922 to 1934 indicate that Ur was at the height of its prosperity from about 2070 to about 1960 B.C., when it was destroyed by invading Amorites. Ur was rebuilt by rulers of the Old Babylonian Dynasty and was subsequently occupied by Neo-Babylonian, or Chaldean, kings. Cyrus the Persian made repairs on the walls of Ur, but the city was abandoned shortly after. It may be that a change in the course of the Euphrates caused the inhabitants of Ur to seek a new location. Terah and Abraham were heirs of the great Sumerian culture of Ur. With the promise of spiritual blessing, they became pilgrims leaving the civilized but idolatrous Sumerian city for the land of God's promise, Canaan.

Haran. Following the migration from Ur, Terah and his family settled in Haran, a northern Mesopotamian city, which like Ur, was devoted to the worship of the moon-god. Terah was content to remain in Haran but Abraham, mindful of the call of God, moved on toward Canaan.

The region around Haran continued to be recognized as the ancestral home of the family of Abraham. It was known as Paddan-aram ("Field of Aram") or Aram-naharaim ("Aram of the Two Rivers").

Haran, or Harran, as it is spelled in the cuneiform literature, was an important trading center during the nineteenth and eighteenth centuries before Christ. The name is similar, although not identical in the original, to that of a brother of Abraham. The literature of the Patriarchal Age also mentions a town of Nahor (also a brother of Abraham), Til-Turakhi (Terah) and Sarugi (Serug).

Amorites. The Sumerians, who lived in southern Mesopotamia when history began in that region (c. 3000 B.C.), chose to live in city-states ruled by a representative of the local god. As in the case of Greece two-and-a-half millennia later, the Sumerians were not prepared to meet the challenge of empire builders. About the middle of the third millennium, a Semite known as Sargon of Accad conquered the Sumerian states and carved out an empire extending to the Mediterranean. Although the Sumerians staged a remarkable comeback, Semitic influence continued to grow.

Early in the second millennium virtually all of Mesopotamia fell into the hands of Semitic peoples called Amorites, or "Westerners." Assyria was governed by the Amorite, Shamshi-Adad I (c. 1727-1695 B.C.) whose sons were trained to succeed him as efficient rulers. The Amorite capital at Mari, on the middle Euphrates, was excavated by Andrè Parrot. Twenty thousand clay tablets discovered there have proved an important source of information concerning the Patriarchal Age. Dealing with military, administrative and diplomatic matters, they illustrate the mobility which characterized the Amorite world of the late eighteenth century. The king of Assyria, from his capital at Assur on the Tigris, negotiated with the king of Qatna, in central Syria, for the marriage of his son with the latter's daughter reminiscent of Abraham's quest for a bride for Isaac. Assyrian merchants established trading communities in Cappadocia, Asia Minor, where commercial transactions with the homeland were maintained. The movement of the Biblical Patriarchs can be appreciated as a part of a manner of life in which mobility formed an important factor.

The term Amorite was originally used of all the peoples who spoke the dialects which grammarians term Northwest Semitic. This included the peoples whom we know as Aramaeans and Hebrews. In later use, however, the term came to be applied to groups of inhabitants of Palestine with which the Israelites came into conflict. In Egyptian records dating about 1300 B.C., all of northern Palestine is called "the land of the Amorites."

The Mari tablets contain names which suggest familiar Biblical parallels. The Mari *Abam-ram* approximates the Biblical Abraham and *Jacob-el* is similar to Jacob. An Amorite tribe of Benjamites is frequently mentioned, although the relation to the Biblical tribe of that name is purely a verbal one. A troublesome group at Mari was known as the Hapiru, equated by many scholars with the Biblical term "Hebrew." The Hapiru appear throughout Mesopotamia, Anatolia, Canaan and Egypt. They serve as raiders, mercenary soldiers, captives, government employees and slaves. They are people who are outside the pale of the established societies among which they moved. Thus they were looked upon as a potential threat to the forces of law and order. The term Hapiru was an expression of social status, or its lack. All Hapiru were certainly not Hebrews in the Biblical sense of the term, but Hebrews were doubtless looked upon as Hapiru by the established governments of the day. It is significant that the term Hebrew is rarely used in Scripture, and then almost always when an Israelite seeks to identify himself to a foreigner.

Zimri-Lim of Mari, whose capital was excavated by Parrot, was conquered by another Amorite king, the famous Hammurabi, or Hammurapi, of Babylon. Hammurabi conquered Larsa, Mari and the Assyrian territory of Shamshi-Adad, thus establishing a unified empire which he ruled with wisdom and clemency. His famous law code, written in Semitic Accadian but based on earlier Sumerian antecedents, is an important document in cultural history. It was discovered early in the twentieth century at the Persian city of Susa, where it had been taken by Elamite raiders. Laws for all situations of life from marriage and the care of children to the rights of veterans and the control of river traffic are clearly presented.

Amorite control of Babylon came to an end around 1500 B.C. when the capital city fell to the Cassites, uncultured foreigners whose rule left few remains.

Nuzu. The city of Nuzu, or Nuzi, in northeastern Mesopotamia gives us a detailed description of many of the customs reflected in the Biblical narratives of the Patriarchal Age. The cuneiform tablets from Nuzu were written by Hurrian scribes in the Accadian (Assyro-Babylonian) language. Hurrians are known as Horites to readers of the English Bible.

A large number of Nuzu documents deal with the institution of adoption. As in Israel, land could not be permanently alienated at Nuzu. A legal fiction could be devised, however, in which land and money would become "presents" to those who by adoption are now members of the family! There was no limit to the size of an estate which could be amassed through this means of circumventing the law.

There were, of course, adoptions resulting from higher motives than land seizure. A childless family might desire a means of insuring the continuity of their name and line. The adopted son would properly care for his new parents during their lifetime, and see to it that the mourning rites were properly cared for at their death. Adoption contracts carefully outline the duties and responsibilities of each party involved.

The eventuality of the birth of a natural son into the family was cared for in the Nuzu adoption contracts. The natural son would become the chief heir and the adopted son would take a secondary position. Household gods were highly esteemed in the Nuzu area, and their possession implied the right of headship over the family. Contracts provided that an adopted son would not have title to the household gods after a natural son was born.

Sometimes adoption was related to marriage at Nuzu. A father might "adopt" his daughter's husband, thus insuring that someone would assume the responsibilities of a son for him. Grandchildren, whose descent was legally reckoned through the father, would thus become his legal heirs.

The patriarch Abram complained to God that he had no son (Gen. 15:2), and that his heir was a servant named Eliezer. Abram seems to have adopted his trusted servant, although he longed for a son of his own. God made it clear that Abram would have a son "of his own loins" who would be the true heir.

When Jacob arrived at Paddan-aram it appears that Laban, his uncle, had no son. Jacob married Laban's daughters, Leah and Rachel, and he seems to have been adopted as Laban's son. Subsequently, however, Laban had sons of his own and the favored position of Jacob and his wives came to an end. Jacob, who had been cheated by Laban on several occasions, determined to return to Canaan with the property he acquired in Paddan-aram. Rachel, desirous of securing the principal inheritance for herself and her husband, stole the *teraphim,* or family idols (Gen. 31:19, 34, 35). Laban, learning of Jacob's flight, pursued his caravan, indignantly asking, "Wherefore hast thou stolen my gods?" (Gen. 31:30). The entire epsiode accords with the usage at Nuzu where the heir possesses the household gods.

The conduct of Sarah in urging her husband to have sexual relations with Hagar is inexplicable by modern standards. The Nuzu tablets make it clear that, according to the standards of the day, the prime purpose of marriage was the bearing of children. Marriage contracts specify that a wife who does not produce children is to provide a handmaid through whom children may be born to her husband. The position of the wife is protected in such contracts since they state that the handmaid continues in a servile status even after she has borne children.

The handmaid's children were also protected in that neither they nor their mother could be expelled from the household. After the birth of Ishmael, Hagar was still reckoned as Sarah's handmaid (Gen. 16:6). When, after the birth of Isaac, Sarah wanted Ishmael and his mother expelled, Abraham was grieved and only complied with Sarah's request when given a direct revelation from God (Gen. 21:12).

That Sarah's action in providing Hagar as a handmaid for Abram is not unusual in patriarchal times is clear from the subsequent conduct of Rachel. Unable to bear children herself, she suggested that Jacob have children through Bilhah, her handmaid (Gen. 30:3). It must not be assumed that such arrangements had the sanction of God. Ishmael, the son of Hagar, was specifically rejected in favor of Isaac, the son of Sarah, Abraham's legitimate wife (Gen. 17:18-19).

In the Nuzu tablets an inheritance was considered negotiable, at least within the family. One of the tablets tells of a brother in need of food who sold for three sheep, a grove which he had inherited, a striking parallel to Esau's sale of his birthright for a "mess of pottage."

Oral blessings and covenants form an important element in the earlier Biblical narrative. They are considered binding, even when secured by fraud. When Jacob succeeded in fooling Isaac he received the blessing intended for Esau. Isaac learned of the deceit but he recognized that he had uttered the blessing and could not go back on his word (Gen. 27:23). In a later period, Joshua honored his covenant with the Gibeonites even though it had been made as a result of deception by a potential foe of Israel (Josh. 9). Nuzu court records indicate instances where oral "blessings" are upheld in court. The patriarchal attitude toward the sanctity of the spoken word is thus seen as characteristic of the northern Mesopotamian area of Nuzu.

The Call of Abraham. With Abraham, Old Testament history becomes particularistic in scope. The records from creation to the flood are concerned with mankind. With the call of Abraham attention is focused upon one branch of the human race. The land of Canaan was promised to Abraham and his "seed" or posterity. Abraham is said to have "believed" God, accepting the promises by faith when he was a sojourner in the land of Canaan. Through Abraham witness was made to the true God as opposed to the idolatry which characterized the most highly civilized of societies in the ancient Near East.

The Line of Promise. The Biblical records indicate the blessing of God upon the promised line, or "seed." In the Book of Genesis this begins in a personal way, and then proceeds to a tribal emphasis. It may be outlined as follows:

> Abraham
> Isaac (not Ishmael)
> Jacob (not Esau)
> The Twelve Tribes, or sons, of Jacob

The theocratic position of the tribes becomes more specialized than the rather general promises to Abraham, Isaac and Jacob. Thus Judah is designated as the royal tribe and, later,

Levi becomes the tribe associated with the priesthood. Joseph, the favorite of Jacob, became two tribes when his sons Ephraim and Manasseh were adopted by their grandfather.

Earliest Inhabitants of Palestine. When the Patriarchs entered Palestine, they were not faced with an ethnic vacuum. Various tribes inhabited the land. But before we note the tribes of the patriarchal period, a word about earlier inhabitants is in order.

Some of the earliest human remains have been discovered in caves excavated at Mount Carmel overlooking the Maritime Plain and the Mediterranean. In the absence of written material, however, we cannot say much about the history of these early peoples.

Scripture refers to several peoples who were in Palestine before the arrival of the Biblical Patriarchs. These include:

1. *Rephaim.* The Rephaim were aboriginal giants who lived in Canaan, Edom, Moab and Ammon. Og, king of Bashan at the time of the Exodus, was "of the remnant of the Rephaim" (Deut. 3:11). A fertile valley running southwest from Jerusalem to Bethlehem bears the name of this people: the Valley of Rephaim. Daniel, the hero of the Ugaritic tablets discovered in northern Syria at Ras Shamra in 1929, is called "the Man of Repha," doubtless an allusion to his tribe. Rephaim are frequently mentioned in the administrative tablets of Ugarit.

The term Rephaim has the dual meaning of "strong ones" and "ghosts" or "shades of the dead." Although little is known concerning the people named Rephaim, there can be no doubt of their important place in the primitive history of Palestine.

2. *Zuzim or Zamzummim* occupied the eastern plateau south of Bashan and Gilead. Their capital at the time of Abraham (Gen. 14:5) was Ham, thought by some to be Rabbath Ammon. They were displaced by the Ammonites and they early dropped from the pages of history.

3. *Emim* were located south of the Zuzim in the area east of the Dead Sea. Their land was later occupied by the Moabites.

4. *Horim, Horites or Hurrians* lived on Mount Seir in Edom whence they were dispossessed by Esau (Gen. 36:21, 29). Many scholars identify the Biblical Horites with the Hurrians, a non-Semitic people who entered northern Mesopotamia and the eastern highlands from an Indo-Iranian source. By the second millennium before Christ they were spread over much of the Middle East. W. F. Albright believes that the Hurrians originated south of the Caucasus, appearing in the Zagros region about 2400 B.C. The Hurrians were conquered by the Hittites (c. 1370 B.C.) and their land fell to Assyria (c. 1250 B.C.).

5. *Avim* lived in the Shephelah between the Philistine plain and the mountains of Judea (Deut. 2:23; Josh. 13:2, 3). They were conquered by the Caphtorim, or Cretans, who were related to the Philistines.

6. *Anakim.* Hebron was the home of the Anakim, who called it Kirjath-arba. Their gigantic stature struck terror to the Israelite spies during the wilderness wandering (Num. 13). They were conquered by Caleb (Josh. 14) but remnants of the Anakim mingled with the Philistines of the coastal plain. Goliath and his brothers, of the Anakim line, lived as late as the time of David (I Sam. 17:4; II Sam. 21:15-22).

Tribes of the Patriarchal Age. The aboriginal tribes were either extinct or were in a minority in patriarchal times. Important peoples in the land were:

1. *Canaanites.* All of the tribes of Canaan are sometimes called Canaanites. Specialized terms came to be used, however, for Canaanites settled in specific regions. Canaanites are thought to have come from the northeastern part of Arabia about 3000 B.C. By that date a number of important Canaanite cities had already been built, including Jebus (Jerusalem), Megiddo, Byblos (Gebal), Gezer, Hamath and Beth-shan. The Israelite spies reported, "The people be strong that dwell in the land, and the cities are walled, and very great" (Num. 13:28). After the conquest of Canaan by Israel and the arrival of Philistine invaders in southwest Palestine, the Canaanites were restricted to the coastal strip of north Palestine and

southern Syria which the Greeks called Phoenicia. The Phoenician Canaanites settled numerous Mediterranean islands and Carthage in North Africa. The Canaanite fertility cult and human (particularly infant) sacrifice were particularly objectionable to the prophets of Israel. Some Canaanites, notably Rahab and the Gibeonites, were permitted to dwell among the Israelites.

2. *Philistines.* Emigrants from the Aegean region, particularly Crete (Amos 9:7), Philistines had settled in southern Palestine before the Patriarchal Age. Gerar was the principal Philistine city at this early period. It appears to have controlled a rich caravan route and to have enjoyed a comfortable standard of living. During the twelfth century B.C. a body of "Sea Peoples" bound for Egypt was repulsed by Rameses III. They settled instead in what became the land of Philistia, the southern part of the Maritime Plain extending from Joppa to Gaza. The Philistines were non-Semitic, hence "uncircumcised." They had a monopoly of iron in Palestine until the time of David (I Sam. 13:19-22). The Philistines were governed by the "lords" of their five cities, Ashdod, Ashkelon, Ekron, Gath and Gaza. They oppressed Israel during the time of the Israelite judges and probably spurred the desire for kingship in Israel. Under David and Solomon they were made tributary to Israel, but they were never permanently subjugated. Gaza fell to Alexander the Great in 332 B.C. after a long siege. The Philistines ultimately were absorbed by other peoples and passed from history.

3. *Hittites.* The great center of Hittite culture was Asia Minor where two important periods of Hittite dominance are known. The Old or Proto-Hittite Kingdom lasted from about 1600 to 1450 B.C. A better documented New Kingdom lasted from c. 1370 B.C. to 1200 B.C. The Aegean Sea peoples brought about the downfall of the Hittites of Asia Minor. Sargon II took the city of Carchemish on the Euphrates, a Syrian Hittite center, in the eighth century B.C., bringing Hittite history to an end.

Hittites were non-Semites, probably Aryans who crossed the Caucasus Mountains into Armenia and Cappadocia. They are frequently mentioned in the Old Testament narrative. Abraham had dealings with Ephron the Hittite in the Hebron area (Gen. 23:10-20). Hittites are said to have lived in the mountains of Canaan (Num. 13:29). Esau married Hittite wives (Gen. 26: 34).

4. *Girgashites.* Little is known of the Girgashites, who seem to have lived in the region west of the Sea of Galilee (Josh. 24: 11). They were probably absorbed by the surrounding tribes.

5. *Hivites.* In the time of Jacob, Shechem was a principal Hivite city (Gen. 34:2). At the time of Joshua's conquest of Canaan several Hivite towns north of Jerusalem, including the city of Gibeon, made a peace treaty with Joshua (Josh. 9:3-15). The term "Hivite" may be a variant of the Horites, or Hurrian people.

6. *Perizzites.* Nothing is definitely known concerning the Perizzites. Their name implies that they were villagers. It has been suggested that they were Hittite ironworkers living in towns of Canaan or villagers from southern Palestine. They were identified as late as the return from Babylonian captivity (Ezra 9:1).

7. *Jebusites.* The term Jebusite is used of the Canaanites who dwelt in Jerusalem, which bore the name Jebus during the period of their occupation. A Jebusite king was slain by Joshua (Josh. 10:1-27), but the Jebusites occupied Jerusalem until the time of David (Judg. 1:21; II Sam. 5).

8. *Amorites.* One of the most powerful of the peoples of Canaan was the Amorite, a term occasionally used as a synonym for the Canaanite (cf. Gen. 15:16). When the two are distinguished, the Amorite is described as dwelling in the "hill country" and the Canaanite on the coastal plain of the Mediterranean and in the Jordan Valley (Num. 13:29).

In the third millennium B.C., Syria and Palestine were called by the Babylonians "The land of the Amorites." Aggressive Amorites conquered almost all of Mesopotamia early in the second millennium B.C. Assyria was governed by the Amorite, Shamshi-Adad I (1727-1695 B.C.). The famous Babylonian lawgiver, Hammurabi, came from an Amorite background, as did Sihon, the ruler of Heshbon who attacked Israel during the wilderness wandering. A more extensive discussion of the Amorites appears earlier in this chapter.

Israel in Egypt. Egypt touches the southern border of Canaan, and relations between the two lands may be traced to earliest times. Abraham is said to have gone into Egypt during a time of famine in Canaan, and similar situations arose periodically. Palestine is dependent on a rather scanty rainfall, whereas Egypt, until construction of the Aswan Dam, has been irrigated by an annual overflow of the banks of the Nile.

Sold into Egypt by his jealous brethren, Joseph quickly rose to a position of influence. After a period of testing in prison, as a result of false accusation, Joseph became vizier, or prime minister, of Egypt. During a period of famine in the Near East, Egypt had ample food supplies with the result that people came from Palestine to Egypt in order to secure grain. Under these circumstances Joseph's brethren came to Egypt. At the time of their second visit Joseph made himself known to them and instructed them to bring their father Jacob and settle in the land of Goshen, east of the Nile Delta. During the lifetime of Joseph, his father and brothers were happily settled in Goshen, but difficulties arose in the years after his death.

TOPICS

The Sojourn in Egypt	Kadesh-barnea
The Oppression	Sihon and Og
The Exodus	Balaam
The Wandering	Settlement in Transjordan
At Sinai	Death of Moses

CHAPTER 6

EGYPT AND THE EXODUS

The Sojourn in Egypt. During the period when Joseph served as vizier of Egypt, Jacob and his remaining sons settled in the district of Goshen called, by anticipation, "the land of Rameses" (Gen. 47:11). About seventy Israelites entered Egypt (Gen. 46:26, 27; Acts 7:14) where they followed a pastoral life similar to that which the Patriarchs pursued in Canaan. They did not intermix with the Egyptians but formed their own homogeneous society. Proximity to the Egyptians, however, doubtless enabled the Israelites to learn new agricultural techniques and Egyptian arts and crafts which would prove useful after Israel re-entered Canaan.

The Oppression. The Israelites probably entered Egypt during the reign of the Hyksos ("rulers of foreign lands"), a group of Asiatics, largely of Semitic extraction, who had invaded Egypt and seized the government there (c. 1720 B.C.). Under a native Egyptian, Ahmose, the Hyksos were expelled (c. 1550 B.C.) and a new dynasty was established.

As might be expected, the native Egyptians looked with suspicion on the Semitic Israelites and feared they might prove disloyal in the event of further warfare. Thus Israel was enslaved and measures were taken to prevent their numerical growth. As Israel prayed for deliverance, God raised up Moses who, following a series of plagues which showed the weakness of the gods of Egypt, led Israel out of the land.

The Exodus. Agreement on the date of the Exodus is lacking. In general two periods are suggested: 1. An "early date" during the fifteenth century (c. 1440 B.C.); 2. A "late date" during the thirteenth century (several are suggested).

The chief argument for the early date is based on I Kings 6:1 which states that Solomon began building the Temple in the four hundred and eightieth year after the Exodus from Egypt. The fourth year of Solomon's reign, when the Temple was built, was about 962 B.C. Thus, if the 480 years are taken literally, the Exodus took place around 1442 B.C. The Pharaoh of this time was Thutmose III, an Egyptian ruler who is known for his building operations and his employment of Semitic slave labor. Ahmose, who expelled the Hyksos, would qualify as the "new king over Egypt who knew not Joseph" (Exod. 1: 8), and the Israelites, arriving in Canaan about 1400 B.C. could be identified with the Hapiru who were threatening Palestinian cities of that period, according to the Tell el-Amarna tablets from fourteenth-century Egypt.

The "late date," however, also has impressive evidence. Exodus 1:11 states that the Israelite laborers "built for Pharaoh store cities, Pithom and Raamses." These cities are located in the Delta where Pharaohs of the Rameside age (the reigns of the Pharaohs named Rameses) resided, and where the Israelites lived and worked. The earlier building projects of Thutmose III seem to have been centered in the southern part of the country. Raamses is probably to be identified with *Per Ramesese,* "the house of Rameses," which has been identified with Avaris or Tanis. The Pharaoh suggested by adherents to the "late date" is Rameses II. According to this view the Exodus probably took place about 1290 B.C. and the entrance into Palestine about 1250 B.C.

Conclusive evidence for the date of the Exodus is not available. The 480-year period (I Kings 6:1) may be a round number for twelve generations (twelve × forty years) which would not argue for an exact chronology. The date of the fall of Jericho (c. 1400 B.C.), earlier suggested by Garstang, has been rejected by his successor in the excavation work at Jericho, Kathleen Kenyon.

The Wandering. After crossing the Red Sea (more literally, "Reed Sea," probably one of the lakes of the Isthmus of Suez), Israel moved southward into the Sinai Peninsula. This was a circuitous route, to be sure, but a theological reason for it is given: God "did not lead them by way of the land of the Philistines, although that was near," but rather led them "by the way of the wilderness" (Exod. 13:17, 18). The presence of Philistines on the coastal route would have meant warfare, and Israel was not yet ready for large-scale battle operations. The wilderness provided a training ground on which God revealed Himself to Israel (notably at Sinai) and prepared His people for entrance into Canaan. Although a generation perished in the wilderness, Joshua brought the second generation into the land of promise.

At Sinai. Sinai, or Horeb, is probably to be located in the southern part of the Sinai Peninsula. It is significant as the place where the Law was given to Israel, the priesthood consecrated, and the Tabernacle erected. Sinai was the place where Israel covenanted to be faithful to the Lord and He rehearsed His past faithfulness as evidence of His continuing mercy. The covenant at Sinai marked Israel as the people of God. In subsequent years they frequently broke the covenant, and the hand of God in chastisement came upon a rebellious people.

Kadesh-barnea. From Kadesh-barnea, about seventy miles south of Hebron, Israelite spies were sent to reconnoiter the land of Canaan. Spies from all of the tribes agreed that the land was good, but only two, Caleb and Joshua, were willing to press on to occupy the land. The ten other spies were frightened at the powerful walled cities and the gigantic stature of their inhabitants. The "evil report" of the ten was accepted, and Israel spent a generation in the wilderness unwilling and unable to occupy their promised land (Num. 14:6-10, 40-45).

Sihon and Og. At the close of the period of wandering, Israel marched around Edom and Moab, and into the country of Sihon, king of the Amorites, who sought to prevent them from passing through his country. At Jahaz, Sihon was defeated in a battle which was decisive. The report of it struck terror in the hearts of the inhabitants of Canaan (Num. 21: 21-31; cf. Josh. 2:10, 11). A second battle with Og, king of Bashan, at Edrei, established the military position of Israel east of the Jordan (Num. 21:33-35).

Balaam. The Moabites and their allies, fearful of the growing power of Israel, determined to check them by the use of magic. The king of Moab sent to Pethor in northern Mesopotamia to secure the services of a famed soothsayer who might be prevailed upon to pronounce a curse on Israel. Balaam was desirous of pleasing his employers, but when he opened his mouth to curse Israel he could only utter a blessing instead (Num. 24:5-9).

Although his magic did not avail, Balaam wrought harm on the camp of Israel in another way. He suggested that the Moabites invite the Israelites to take part in their fertility cult worship at Baal-peor. There Israel was introduced to the fatally attractive rite of cult prostitution which formed one of the most obnoxious parts of Canaanite religion. This orgy of licentiousness brought about a divine judgment on Israel. God did not, however, blot out His people, as Balaam doubtless desired (Num. 31:8, 15, 16).

Settlement in Transjordan. The tribes of Reuben and Gad and half the tribe of Manasseh looked upon the rich pasture-land of Transjordan as suitable for their herds and flocks. Requesting permission to settle there, Moses insisted that the men cross the Jordan and assist in the conquest of Canaan before entering their lands east of the Jordan.

Death of Moses. Somewhere in the hill country designated Mount Nebo, Moses was buried after having viewed the land of promise from the mountains of Moab, dying at a ripe, old age with eye not dim nor natural force abated.

CHAPTER 7

THE CONQUEST OF CANAAN

AFTER SPENDING A GENERATION in the wilderness, Israel was ready to enter Canaan and lay claim to the territory which had once been the home of the Patriarchs. Moses had brought the people out of Egypt, given them the Law, and provided political and military leadership during the years subsequent to the Exodus.

The victories over Sihon and Og in the Transjordan country formed a prelude to victories which would follow in the Promised Land. Moses, however, did not live to lead his people into western Palestine. Joshua, who had served as Moses' "minister" and associate, was appointed to lead Israel into Canaan before Moses died on the plains of Moab.

Crossing the Jordan. The sojourn in the Sinai Peninsula began when God caused "a strong east wind" to hold back the waters of the Red (Reed) Sea. At the close of the period of

47

wandering, the Jordan River was miraculously held back in order to permit the Israelites to cross on dry ground.

Although Scripture does not indicate the means used in holding back the Jordan waters, it is stated (Josh. 3:16) that they were piled up at a specific place quite far removed from the actual place of crossing. This suggests that an earthquake produced a landslide of sufficient magnitude to dam up the Jordan for a time sufficient to permit Israel to cross. On other known occasions landslides have cut off the Jordan waters. In 1927, an earthquake collapsed a 150-foot cliff, causing the waters to be stopped for twenty-one and one-half hours.

Powerful city-states of Canaan maintained armies which might have been expected to resist the Israelite crossing. Military intelligence would assume, however, that a fording would take place during the low water season. The Jordan was in flood stage when its waters were held back, permitting Israel to enter Canaan unchallenged.

Gilgal. One of several Old Testament towns bearing the name of Gilgal (lit., "a circle of stones," from the root "to roll") was the site of Israel's first encampment in Canaan. Here twelve stones taken from the Jordan were erected as a monument to God's faithfulness (Josh. 4:1-9, 20).

Gilgal marks a period of transition for Israel. Joshua was the acknowledged leader. The miraculous manna which had provided sustenance during the wilderness wandering ceased and Israel began to acquire its food by natural (although, of course, providential) means. The rite of circumcision which appears to have been neglected during the wilderness period, was reestablished, and the Passover was celebrated.

The Central Campaign (Jericho). The military strategy in the conquest of Canaan was designed to divide the country, and then conquer the southern and northern sectors. The key to Canaan was the walled city of Jericho in central Palestine, just north of the place where the Jordan River empties into the Dead Sea.

Jericho was strongly fortified, and the Israelites were largely untrained, just emerging from an undisciplined existence in the wilderness. Previously they had been slaves in Egypt. Yet Jericho fell before Israel. Scripture indicates that the victory was a supernatural one. The walls fell, presumably during one of the earthquakes which are quite common in the region. From the Biblical point of view nature is not separated from God but rather is the means of His operation. God brought about the destruction of Jericho. Rahab, who had protected Israelite spies when they came to investigate the nature of enemy territory, was spared, together with her household. The city and its inhabitants, however, were offered as a kind of "first fruits" sacrifice, devoted to the God of Israel.

Jericho has been the site of extensive archaeological work. In 1908 two German scholars, Sellin and Watzinger, began to work there. An English expedition directed by John Garstang worked at the site from 1930 to 1936. Since 1952, a series of excavations sponsored by the British School of Archaeology and the American School of Oriental Research has been directed by Miss Kathleen Kenyon.

Earlier reports concerning discoveries of the Jericho of Joshua's day have been largely discredited. Although we may now not assert dogmatically which of the walls fell in the attack, the Biblical text informs us that it was a powerful, walled city which was the first city of Canaan to fall before Joshua.

Shortly after the conquest of Jericho, attack was made on a place known to us as Ai (literally, "the ruin"). A mound known as Et-Tell (literally, "the mound" a synonym for Ai) was excavated in 1933-34 by Mme. Judith Marquet-Kraus. According to archaeological remains it was a flourishing city between 3300 and 2400 B.C., after which it was destroyed, never again to become a city of importance. During the period between 1200 and 1000 B.C. it was occupied by a few Israelites.

In view of the fact that no account is given of the conquest of Bethel, only a mile and a half from Ai, some scholars infer that the battle of Ai was actually a battle for Bethel. Father

Hugues Vincent suggests that Ai may have been a military out-
post for Bethel. It is, of course, possible that the equation of
Et-Tell with Ai is incorrect and that subsequent discoveries will
throw more light on this phase of history.

The Southern Campaign.   Israelite victories at Jericho
and Ai struck terror in the hearts of the Canaanites. Most of
them prepared to defend themselves but one group, the Gibeonites, determined to make an alliance with Israel as a means
of self-preservation. Feigning themselves travelers from a distant country, they succeeded in tricking Joshua into making
an alliance which was honored even when the deceit was de-
tected.

The leaders of the city-states of Southern Canaan were unwilling to sit by while the power of Israel became greater.
Adonizedek of Jerusalem, with the kings of Hebron, Jarmuth,
Lachish and Eglon, marched against Gibeon. The Gibeonites
appealed to Joshua for aid. He staged a hasty night march
from the camp at Gilgal and came upon the kings from south
Canaan in their encampment near Gibeon at daybreak.

Joshua's attack was successful. The armies of the southern
coalition fled down the western slope of the hill past Beth-
horon. A hailstorm killed many of the fleeing Canaanites. The
remainder continued their flight down the Valley of Ajalon as
far as Makkedah. There the five kings were trapped and slain.

The Book of Joshua, in describing these events, quotes an
earlier source, the Book of Jasher. Like many nations of antiquity, Israel commemorated her early victories in a form
known to us as epic poetry. Poetry is easier to remember than
prose, and the epics were passed on orally from generation to
generation. Although we could not prove that the Book of
Jasher was passed on orally before reduced to writing, we do
know that quotations from it in the Bible are all poetic in form.

The quotation from the Book of Jasher (Josh. 10:12, 13)
describes the event generally known as "Joshua's long day,"
during which the Israelites succeeded in completing the destruc-

tion of the southern armies. The traditional view that the day was actually prolonged need not involve a stopping of the solar system. Lengthened hours of daylight may have been brought about by refraction, or some other means unknown to us.

A number of writers, including R. D. Wilson, E. W. Maunder and Hugh Blair, interpret the words "stood still" as meaning "ceased to shine." The miracle, according to this suggestion, would be one of prolonged darkness rather than prolonged light. It is suggested that the Israelites had staged a surprised attack under cover of darkness, gaining the initiative against the Canaanites. Prolonged darkness and a hailstorm enabled Israel to work havoc in the camp of the enemy. Those who hold to this view translate the words commonly rendered "the sun . . . hasted not to go down about a whole day," as "the sun hasted not to come about a whole day."

Other conservative scholars, including Keil, Kurz and Hengstenberg, stress the poetic nature of the passage and do not seek to explain it literally. It is compared with Judges 5:20, "The stars in their courses fought against Sisera." This is a poetic way of stating that God used all of the forces of nature to accomplish the defeat of Israel's foes.

The miraculous intervention of God is asserted in Joshua 10:14: "There was no day like that before it or after it, that the Lord hearkened unto the voice of a man: for the Lord fought for Israel." The Biblical writers were certain that the battles fought with Canaanites were the subject of God's special providence, and that victory could be accounted for only on the grounds of God's intervention on behalf of His people.

The Northern Campaign. Following the victory over the southern Canaanites, the army of Israel returned to its encampment at Gilgal. One important area was yet untouched by Joshua's armies, and the tide of battle moved in that direction.

Jabin, king of the powerful city-state of Hazor in northern Canaan, determined to lead a resistance movement which might check the progress of Israel. So great was the Israelite threat that Jabin had no difficulty in enlisting the help of other city-states and ethnic groups of northern Canaan. This Hazor Confederacy, as it is frequently termed, grouped its forces in the vicinity of the Waters of Merom for a showdown battle with Joshua. Older maps identified the Waters of Merom with Lake Huleh, north of the Sea of Galilee, but more recent studies indicate a location southwest of Hazor.

Joshua took the offensive and launched a surprise attack, his usual technique on the field of battle. The Hazor Confederacy fled, pursued by Joshua as far as Sidon, on the Phoenician coast. This victory for Israel, following that at Jericho and over the southern Canaanites, completed the conquest of Canaan. Many areas were by-passed and resistance continued from some sectors until the time of David, but the initial phase of the occupation of the land was completed with the destruction of Hazor and its allies.

The smaller cities "that stood on their mounds" (Josh. 11: 13) were spared and doubtless used by Israelite settlers. Hazor itself, however, was completely destroyed. Its strategic importance has been underscored by excavations of the city identified in 1926 by Garstang, and carefully excavated by an Israelite expedition which began work in 1955 under the direction of Yigael Yadin.

The area occupied by Hazor comprised nearly 200 acres, with a population estimated at 40,000. Joshua destroyed the chariotry, which Hazor used as the backbone of its attack. Chariots, made of wood, were burned, and horses were hamstrung (i.e., disabled by cutting the tendon of the joint in the hind leg). In this way they were rendered unfit for warfare, but they might still be used domestically. Israel did not use chariots in Joshua's day, and it appears that horses were regarded as a source of temptation. Israel might trust in horses instead of placing her trust in the Lord.

Unconquered Territory.   Joshua may be regarded as one of the world's great military figures. He combined faith in God with military genius in accomplishing feats of battle which would be considered impossible under normal circumstances.

Yet, when he reached old age, there remained "very much land to be possessed" (Josh. 13:1). The Philistines occupied the land along the Mediterranean coast from the Brook of Egypt (*Wadi el-Arish*) to Joppa. They continued as a thorn in Israel's side until the reign of David, and did not completely disappear until Judas Maccabeus inflicted a crushing defeat on them.

Phoenician cities such as Sidon and Gebal (Byblos) represent another group that did not fall before the armies of Joshua. David and Solomon had friendly relations with the Phoenicians. Hiram of Tyre provided both materials and artisans for their building operations.

The Division of the Land. In dividing Canaan among the tribes, Joshua both recognized the victories given by God and encouraged the tribes to enter and occupy the land assigned to them.

Judah was assigned the territory of southern Canaan, east and southeast of the Dead Sea. A part of this land was subsequently assigned to Simeon because "the part of the children of Judah was too much for them" (Josh. 19:1-9).

The important central part of Canaan was assigned to the Joseph tribes—Ephraim and Manasseh. This was a rich and fertile section, but Canaanite fortresses at Beth-shan, Ibleam, Dor, Taanach and Megiddo proved a barrier to the occupation of the area. Ephraim and Manasseh complained about the inadequacy of their assigned portion, only to be assured by Joshua that they could conquer the Canaanites "though they have chariots of iron, and though they be strong" (Josh. 17:11-18).

Between the land assigned to Judah and that of the Joseph tribes was territory assigned to Benjamin (Josh. 18:11-28) and Dan (Josh. 19:40-48). At the border between Judah and Benjamin was the city of the Jebusites, later to become the spiritual and political center of united Israel. The tribe of Dan had difficulty in maintaining itself in the coastal area where the Amorites were strong (Judg. 1:34). A group of Danites migrated to the extreme northern sector of Canaan. It is from this northern Dan that the borders of Israel are delineated: "from Dan to Beersheba."

The tribes of Asher, Zebulun, Issachar and Naphtali received inheritances in the north (Josh. 19:10-39). Reuben, Gad and half the tribe of Manasseh had already received an inheritance east of the Jordan (Num. 32:1-42; Josh. 13:7-33).

The Levites, whose concern was the public worship of the Lord, were not given a tribal inheritance. Instead they were assigned forty-eight cities with the suburbs, or pasture-land, of each. These cities were scattered among the tribes. Included among them were six "cities of refuge," three on each side of the Jordan, set apart as an asylum for those who had committed unintentional homicide. If a fugitive could convince the elders of the city that he did not have murderous intent, he stood trial before the entire assembly. When declared innocent, the fugitive was permitted to remain within the city of refuge until the death of the high priest. Then he could return home without fear of an avenger of the blood of the slain man.

CHAPTER 8

WHEN THE JUDGES JUDGED

THE BOOK OF JOSHUA indicates that the conquest of Canaan was far from complete at the time of the division of the land among the tribes. Important confederations of Canaanites from the southern and northern parts of the land had been conquered, but there were major pockets of resistance which challenged the right of Israel to the land as late as the time of Saul.

Events following the death of Joshua are recorded in the Book of Judges. There we are told of a series of national calamities in which the enemies of Israel gained control of the land, and of the "judges" who were raised up by God to deliver His people.

The Term "Judge." The judges had a much wider sphere of service than the English term denotes. The term might better be rendered "savior" or "deliverer." Judges were military figures, leading the armies of Israel against her enemies. They also had civil functions, serving as rulers of the people in the absence of an earthly king. In theory at least, God was the true King of His people.

The judges did not form dynasties, as did the later kings. Tendencies in this direction are discernible in the case of Gideon and Samuel, whose sons were thought of as potential successors to their gifted fathers. During the period of the judges, however, individuals were raised up by God to meet particular crises without regard to dynastic succession. The judges are frequently termed *charismatic,* i.e., "gifted," rulers. Enabled by God to deliver His people from the oppressor, the judge occupied a place of influence during the remainder of his lifetime. No successor was indicated, however, and future crises demanded the call and empowering of a new "judge."

The Philosophy of History. From the time of her entrance into Canaan, Israel was subject to temptation. Canaanite fertility rites appeared to be a valid means of securing good crops, and many Israelites copied the practices of their neighbors. This was, however, a violation of the covenant made at Mount Sinai with the Lord, who declared Himself to be a jealous God who could tolerate no rival.

The Book of Judges records a series of seven apostasies from the Lord. After each, we read that the God of Israel delivered His people into the hands of an enemy. In their affliction, Israel prayed for deliverance, with the result that a "judge" or deliverer was raised up to meet the crisis. After the deliverance, the judge continued to reign until his death, after which apostasy again took place. Another round of humiliation, prayer and deliverance would then take place. The author of the Book of Judges wished to show that disobedience to God brought defeat to His people. The mercy of God is underscored, however, in that God hearkens to them when they cry unto Him in their distress.

Characteristics of the Time of the Judges. During the period between the death of Joshua and the anointing of Saul, God was nominal King over His people. In practice, however, "every man did that which was right in his own eyes." There was no central government, tribes functioned alone or in concert with their neighbors. Individuals are spoken of as Ephraimites, Danites or Gileadites (i.e., from the tribes east of the Jordan).

The local nature of the history of the judges makes it probable that some of them may have been contemporary. Samson's activities were in southwestern Canaan, the original Danite country where the Philistines were a constant threat to Israel. Jephthah, on the other hand, was from the east Jordan country of Gilead where he delivered his people from the Ammonites. This fact, plus the use of round numbers (frequently multiples of forty), makes it impossible to establish an exact chronology for the period of the judges.

The Oppressors and Deliverers

Oppressor	Length of Oppression	Judge	Length of Judgeship or Rest from Oppression	Scripture Reference
Cushan-rishathaim of Aram-naharaim (Mesopotamia)	?	Othniel	40 years rest	3:8-11
Eglon of Moab with Ammonites and Amalekites	18 years	Ehud	80 years rest	3:12-30
Philistines	?	Shamgar	?	3:31
Jabin of Canaan, Sisera his captain	?	Deborah with Barak	40 years rest	4:1—5:31
Midianites	7 years	Gideon (Usurpation of Abimelech)	?	6:1—8:28 8:29—9:57
		Tola	23 years	10:1, 2
		Jair	22 years	10:3-5
Ammonites	18 years	Jephthah	6 years	10:6—12:7
		Ibzan	7 years	12:8-10
		Elon	10 years	12:11, 12
		Abdon	8 years	12:13-15
Philistines	40 years	Samson	20 years	13:1—16:31

The Civil Wars. Tribal and intertribal tensions produced three crises which may be termed civil wars.

1. *The Usurpation of Abimelech.* Although Gideon refused to be named as a hereditary king, his son, Abimelech, gained the support of his mother's family, killed his brothers and seized the throne. A brother, Jotham, escaped and delivered the Parable of the Trees (Judg. 9), indicating contempt for the institution of kingship. According to Jotham, trees doing worthwhile things such as producing figs or olives could not be bothered with the responsibilities of kingship. Only the worthless bramble aspired to lord it over others. Subsequently Abimelech was killed when a woman from Thebez threw an upper millstone on his head. Thus the abortive attempt to establish kingship in Israel was ended.

2. *The War between the Gileadites and the Ephraimites.* When Jephthah led the Gileadites against the Ammonites, the tribe of Ephraim did not take part. Angered at not being able to share in the spoil, they expressed dissatisfaction with Jephthah's policy. War ensued, with terrific casualties for the Ephraimites who were slain at the fords of the Jordan. The incident illustrates the dialectical differences which were current among the tribes, for the Ephraimites were unable to pronounce the word "shibboleth," used by the Gileadites as a password. In the Ephraimite dialect the sound which we represent as "sh" was pronounced "s"—hence the pronunciation "sibboleth" which identified them as enemies.

3. *War with the Benjaminites.* The mistreatment and slaying of a Levite's concubine by a Benjaminite, who was subsequently protected by his fellow-tribesmen, produced a rupture among the tribes. All Israel gathered to humble Benjamin, a small tribe which for a time defied the united forces of her neighbors. Through a ruse the Israelites were able to capture Gibeah and almost annihilate the male population of Benjamin. Fearful lest the tribe should perish, special provision was made to provide wives for the surviving Benjaminites.

CHAPTER 9

BEGINNINGS OF THE MONARCHY: SAMUEL AND SAUL

Samuel. A transition figure, bridging the period between the rule of the judges and the establishment of the monarchy, Samuel was judge, prophet and king-maker. He was born of pious parents and raised by Eli, a godly but weak priest, in "the house of the Lord" at Shiloh. The Tabernacle of earlier history seems to have become a more permanent structure after the settlement in Canaan. Shiloh served as its center until the city was destroyed in one of the Philistine raids.

The Philistines, who threatened Israel during the time of the judges, continued as a threat throughout Samuel's lifetime. Early in his career Israel suffered humiliation at Aphek. In order to insure victory, the Israelites brought the Ark to the field of battle, using it as a kind of "good-luck charm." Instead of ending in victory, however, the Battle of Aphek was one of utter humiliation. The Ark was captured, Eli's sons were slain, and the aged priest himself died when he heard news of the catastrophe.

Although the spiritual leadership of Samuel restored Israel to a position of strength, the Philistine menace continued. Sam-

59

uel's sons were not following their godly father. The uncertainties of the situation doubtless fostered a desire for kingship in Israel. Kings were thought of as men of grandeur and power. If Israel was to take a position of prominence among the nations, she too must have a king. This was the logic of the situation.

Samuel recognized the demand for a king as a rejection of his own rule, and that of God Himself. In bringing the matter before the Lord, Samuel was instructed to give the people a king. He eloquently warned the people of the tyranny they might expect, but the people were insistent. The theocracy was ended, and Israel became a monarchy.

Monarchy in Israel. Although one of the motivations in the demand for a king was conformity to the customs of neighboring peoples, kingship in Israel was unique in the ancient world. An Egyptian Pharaoh was regarded as a god who at death returned to his "horizon." An Assyrian or a Babylonian sovereign, although recognized as a mortal, was the darling of the gods who could do no wrong. He was head of "church" as well as "state." His word was law, and there was no check upon his power—except for that check with which all despots must reckon, rebellion and intrigue.

In Israel, however, the king ruled "by the grace of God," in a very real sense. He was anointed by a priest and was not personally permitted to assume priestly prerogatives. The law of God was higher than any man, and the king was expected to respect and obey it.

This was not only a pious idealism but a practical reality. When Saul presumed to offer sacrifice, when David took Uriah's wife and when Ahab seized Naboth's vineyard, judgment was pronounced and executed. The marvel is not that kings in Israel sinned, but that they recognized the right of a Nathan to point the finger of accusation and say, "Thou art the man!"

Saul Begins to Reign. By divine direction Samuel anointed Saul of Benjamin as Israel's first king. Benjamin was the smallest of the tribes, so chances of intertribal jealousy were reduced

when a Benjaminite became ruler. Tall and imposing in appearance, Saul was the kind of impressive king the Israelites had
desired.

Saul's responsibilities were difficult. He had to unite a people
who had been jealous of tribal rights. Weapons were few and
enemies, particularly Philistines, were numerous.

A crisis brought Saul's leadership to the fore. The Ammonites
demanded that the people of Jabesh-gilead submit to the brutal
humiliation of having one eye struck out. Saul, who had been
plowing with a yoke of oxen when he heard the report of Jabesh-gilead, decided to act. He cut up his oxen and sent the
pieces throughout Israel, warning that any who refused to come
to the aid of Jabesh-gilead would have their oxen cut up in like
manner. Saul proved an able leader, and his rescue of Jabesh-
gilead was but the first of a series of Israelite victories.

Rupture with Samuel. Saul's excellent beginning was later
marred by a spirit of impatience and pride. This resulted in a
tendency to act independently, forgetting his dependence upon
the Lord. Samuel's earlier words of warning proved true.

When Samuel had delayed his coming to Michmash, Saul decided to offer the burnt offering personally (I Sam. 13:8-13).
This was clearly an intrusion of the king into priestly matters.
Samuel warned, "Your kingdom shall not continue . . . because
you have not kept what the Lord commanded you" (I Sam. 13:
14).

A second rupture took place when Saul spared Agag and the
sheep and oxen of the Amalekites. Samuel had instructed Saul,
"Smite Amalek and utterly destroy all that they have" (I Sam.
15:3). Saul, when confronted with the evidence of his disobedience, protested that he had spared the best of the Amalekite flocks that he might make a sacrifice to the Lord. Samuel's
reply is memorable: "Has the Lord as great delight in burnt
offerings and sacrifices, as in obeying the voice of the Lord?
Behold, to obey is better than sacrifice, and to hearken than the
fat of rams. For rebellion is as the sin of divination, and stub-
bornness is as iniquity and idolatry. Because you have rejected

the word of the Lord, he has also rejected you from being king" (I Sam. 15:22, 23).

Following his rupture with Samuel, Saul became a tragic character. His latter life is part of the story of David. Insane with jealousy he hunted his supposed rival as if he were a wild beast. David, however, respected "the Lord's anointed" and actually mourned Saul's death at the hands of the Philistines at Mount Gilboa.

CHAPTER 10

DAVID'S RISE — SAUL'S DECLINE

David Secretly Anointed. While Samuel was mourning over the defection of Saul, the Lord directed him to the household of Jesse, a Bethlehemite of the tribe of Judah. In Jesse's house, Samuel recognized David, the youngest son, as the chosen of the Lord. He anointed him in anticipation of the day when he would replace Saul as king over Israel.

David Introduced to Saul. David was first introduced into court life when he served as an armor-bearer for Saul (I Sam. 16:21). His musical ability was of particular help to Saul who seems to have been afflicted with a mental illness which would be termed a manic-depressive psychosis by modern psychologists. In his moments of mental distraction, David's lyre brought refreshment to Saul.

David was at home with his father when his elder brothers were battling the Philistines in the Valley of Elah. Jesse sent

63

David to his brothers with provisions, but the lad stayed to meet the challenge of Goliath of Gath, the Philistine who challenged Israel to send a soldier to meet him in personal combat. David's use of his sling in slaying the "uncircumcised Philistine" is a well-known Biblical story.

David became an immediate hero. In spite of his youth he fought in Saul's armies and became famous for his deeds of courage. The women of Israel sang of his exploits:

> Saul has slain his thousands,
> And David his ten thousands.

Although honoring David, Saul could hardly be expected to be pleased with the unfavorable contrast. Jealousy soon became bitter hatred. Saul determined to kill his rival.

David and Saul's Family. It is one of the ironies of the situation that, although hated by Saul, David had the most cordial relation with members of Saul's family. Jonathan, heir-presumptive to Saul's throne, became David's steadfast friend. Saul's daughter, Michal, lost her heart to the popular young hero, and David sought to learn what marriage present would best satisfy her father. Seeking to use the occasion against David, Saul asked for a hundred foreskins of the Philistines. Proof that enemies were slain usually consisted of heads or hands cut off the victims. Since the Philistines were uncircumcised, Saul demanded their foreskins. Instead of meeting death at the hand of the enemy, as Saul planned, David produced twice the required number of foreskins in half the specified time. He married Michal, a relationship which would later strengthen his claim to the throne in the eyes of the people (I Sam. 18:17-27).

David Flees the Wrath of Saul. David's marriage to his daughter, Michal, only increased Saul's determination to kill him. Jonathan attempted to protect David by warning him of Saul's evil purpose. On one occasion when David was playing his lyre, Saul threw his javelin at David in an attempt to kill him. The javelin hit the wall, and David escaped. On another occasion Saul threw the javelin at his own son when Jonathan attempted to defend David. David fled from Israel, actually taking refuge among the Philistines. He went to Gath where he feigned insanity so that the Philistines would not treat him as an enemy.

David—a Hunted Man. David's flight did not lessen Saul's desire to kill him. Any who showed friendship to David were esteemed enemies of the king. When Saul was persuaded that the priests at Nob were partisans of David, he ordered their massacre. The king's servants would not attack the priests, but Doeg, an Edomite, killed eighty-five of them. Only Abiathar escaped to report the episode to David.

When he learned that David was in the wilderness west of the Dead Sea, Saul and his men pursued as far as to En-gedi. In one instance Saul entered the very cave in which David was hiding. David recognized the king and had him at his mercy, but he would not "lift up his hand" against "the Lord's anointed." He did cut off the skirt of Saul's robe, and subsequently he confronted the king with the fact that he had not taken advantage of the opportunity to kill him. Saul seemed touched by the incident. He wept, asking David not to cut off his name and "house" from Israel.

David and his associates were outlaws in the eyes of Saul, and they had to support themselves by plunder. The incident of Nabal illustrates the means used to secure provisions. David sent ten of his men to convey greetings to Nabal and to collect tribute. Nabal refused to pay, but Abigail his wife went to David with gifts to appease him. David was impressed by Abigail and, after Nabal's death, he married her. The episode illustrates the way a kind of "protection money" might be demanded by a gang of outlaws in the Israel of David's day. David had not molested Nabal, but he felt that he had a rightful claim to tribute from him.

After a further encounter with Saul, in which David again spared the king's life, he fled to Achish, the Philistine king of

Gath. Ironically, David was safer among the Philistines than in his own country. Achish gave the town of Ziklag to David. From Ziklag, David made raids on the foes of Israel but he was careful to spare his own people.

Saul's Desperation. As the Philistines continued to grow in power, Saul's plight became increasingly desperate. The normal means of ascertaining the will of God—through dreams, *urim* or prophets (I Sam. 28:5, 6)—had all failed. Samuel had died, but Saul determined to seek his advice through the aid of a necromancer.

Witchcraft had been outlawed in Israel. Saul himself had attempted to rid the land of those who dealt with "familiar spirits." A witch at Endor had managed to continue her craft and Saul, disguising himself, went to her abode. The encounter was successful, although it boded ill for Saul. The witch herself was surprised when Samuel appeared, identified Saul and assured the king that he would join the departed in *sheol* on the morrow. Scripture does not teach that a spiritist may disturb the dead, but this episode implies that Samuel appeared, perhaps to the surprise of the witch, with a message of judgment.

Philistine Attack on Israel. When the Philistines prepared to attack Israel they excused David, their ally, fearing that he might prove loyal to his own people. Returning to Ziklag, David found that his city had been burned and the women, children, and cattle carried off. David proceeded to organize his forces to rescue property and loved ones. Although some of his troops had to be left behind because of exhaustion, the battle was successful and the victors brought back their property with additional spoils of war. David decreed that all must share alike whether they participated in the battle or served as guards in the rear (I Sam. 30:24).

A crucial battle for Israel was fought at Mount Gilboa. Here the Philistines crushed the Israelite army. Saul and Jonathan were slain and their heads hung on the wall of Beth-shan as a trophy of victory. The men of Jabesh-gilead, remembering how

Saul had once rescued them from the Ammonites, went by night and rescued the bodies of Saul and Jonathan. They were buried with appropriate mourning rites.

An Amalekite brought what he supposed would be welcome news to David. He stated that he had personally killed Saul. David, however, ordered the death of the Amalekite as a regicide. Throughout his career, David did not personally harm one member of the household of Saul. Although he was not immediately to become king over all the tribes, David's attitude toward Saul would one day stand him in good stead with those who might easily have become his enemies.

TOPICS

CHAPTER 11

DAVID AS KING

THE DEATH OF SAUL and Jonathan paved the way for David's assumption of royal prerogatives. Yet David truly mourned the death of the king, his most bitter enemy, and Jonathan, his best freind. One of the most moving poems in all Scripture is the dirge which David composed to express his grief (II Sam. 1:19-27). All nature is invoked to join David in weeping over the loss of two such heroes as Saul and Jonathan. Before it became a part of the Biblical record David's lament was recorded in the poetic Book of Jasher (II Sam. 1:18).

David Anointed King at Hebron. Shortly after the Battle of Mount Gilboa, David returned in safety to Judah and was anointed king in Hebron, about 1000 B.C. The northern tribes, however, were loyal to the house of Saul. Saul's son Esh-baal, or Ish-bosheth, established his capital at Mahanaim, in Transjordan territory. This location was doubtless the result of Philistine dominance in Palestine west of the Jordan. David's earliest years as king may have been spent as their vassal.

The Death of Esh-baal. With Israel divided into two sectors, civil war could be expected. Abner, who had been Saul's general, led the armies of Esh-baal, while Joab served as David's commander. In one encounter Abner killed Asahel, a brother of Joab, with the result that Joab had a personal score to settle with Abner.

Abner foolishly sought to marry Rizpah, one of Saul's concubines. Esh-baal was displeased, for marrying a king's widow was presumptive evidence of a design on the throne. When Esh-baal reprimanded Abner he decided to transfer his allegiance to David. David accepted on condition that Abner see to it that Michal, Saul's daughter, be restored to him as wife. She was torn away from her second husband and married to David, a relationship which proved highly unsatisfactory.

Abner loyally used his influence in turning over the northern tribes to David. Joab, however, treacherously murdered Abner, ostensibly to avenge the death of his brother, Asahel. We suspect, however, that personal jealousy had something to do with it. David mourned over Abner as he had mourned over Saul and Jonathan.

Shortly after the death of Abner we read that Esh-baal, the king of the northern tribes, was murdered and his head brought to David. Again David had the murderers put to death, a fact which enhanced David's reputation in the north.

With the death of Esh-baal the last hindrance to David's assumption of power over all Israel was removed. Yet David had been blameless in all his dealings with the house of Saul. Saul, Esh-baal and Abner were dead, but David had no part in their death and, in the case of Saul and Esh-baal, their murderers were punished by death.

Jerusalem—Capital of United Israel. Upon his accession to the throne of all Israel, David sought a new and more centrally located capital. The city of Jebus was located on the border of Benjamin and Judah, but it was occupied by a group of Canaanites known as Jebusites. Jebus (Jerusalem) had been a prize sought by the Israelites since the time of Joshua, but a permanent foothold there had never been secured.

By stealth, Joab entered Jebus and forced its surrender to David. Jebus became "the city of David" (II Sam. 5:9), or Jerusalem. As Bethlehem is known as the "city of David" because of his birth there, so Jerusalem was the "city of David" because there he reigned as king over all Israel. Since it had not been occupied by either Judah or Benjamin it served as a kind of neutral territory, analogous to the District of Columbia on the border between Maryland and Virginia.

David's Building Plans. With the aid of Phoenician artisans David built a palace in Jerusalem. Desiring to make Jerusalem a spiritual as well as a political center he had the Ark brought there and mentioned to the prophet Nathan his plan to build a temple.

Nathan was pleased with David's plan, but subsequently suggested that it was not God's will that the Temple be built by David, a king whose hands were bloody with war. During the peaceful reign of his son Solomon, a temple would be built.

David's Conquests. From a military viewpoint, David's years following the conquest of Jerusalem were successful. Moab was conquered. The land of the Aramaeans around Damascus was made subject to governors appointed by David. Joab continued as commander of the army. Foreign mercenary troops of Caphtorian origin, Cherethites and Pelethites, served as a kind of personal bodyguard and were subject to Benaiah.

David's magnanimity is seen in his kindness to Meribbaal, or Mephibosheth, the son of Jonathan. Saul's estate was given to Meribbaal and he was supported at government expense. His crippled condition made him no rival for David and also made him and his friends most appreciative of David's clemency.

Bathsheba and Uriah. A turning point in David's life was reached during the siege of Rabbath-ammon. David had remained behind in Jerusalem while his armies were on the field of battle. Having developed an illicit passion for Bathsheba, the wife of one of his soldiers, Uriah the Hittite, David attempted to cover up his crime with her. When Uriah refused to return home to his wife, David gave orders to Joab to send Uriah into the thick of the battle where he would be sure to be killed. The plan was successful. Uriah died in battle, and David married Bathsheba.

Nathan, the prophet of the Lord, brought a message to David. Eloquently describing a rich man who took a poor man's solitary ewe lamb, he appealed to David's sense of justice. When David insisted that the rich man should die, Nathan replied, "Thou art the man."

David accepted Nathan's rebuke. Although his repentance was genuine, there were results which would plague David's later days. The child which was to be born to Bathsheba would die. David's family life would be imperiled, and his own sons would rebel against him.

Domestic Troubles. Amnon, one of David's sons, had illicit relations with his half-sister Tamar. Thereupon Tamar's brother, Absalom, determined to avenge the honor of his sister by slaying Amnon. He then fled to Geshur in Syria, taking refuge with his mother's relations. When Joab noted that the king's heart pined for Absalom he secured the services of a wise woman of Tekoa who presented to the king the imaginary case of a widow, one of whose sons had killed the other. In adjudicating the case for the woman, David saw the wisdom of permitting Absalom to return home. Although not immediately restored to full favor, Absalom soon occupied a place of honor which he abused for his own ends.

The Revolt of Absalom. As David had once been the popular young leader to Saul's discomfiture, so Absalom used his youth and favored position to advance himself. When he had sufficiently gained the loyalty of the people, he had himself crowned king at Hebron with the support of a large part of the people. David was forced to flee from Jerusalem, but Zadok and Abiathar, the priests, remained loyal to him.

As a result of the counsel of Hushai, a friend of David who feigned loyalty to Absalom, David was given opportunity to flee to Mahanaim, east of the Jordan. Hushai counseled Absalom to delay his attack until he had gathered a great army. This afforded David the time to escape and gather his forces. When Absalom and his army crossed the Jordan they were defeated in the "wood of Ephraim," where Absalom himself was caught in a tree and slain by Joab, contrary to David's command. David's grief at the death of his son was so great that Joab had to reprimand him for forgetting that his army had risked life itself to save the king.

Restoration. The ten northern tribes were desirous of David's return to the throne, but Judah remained hesitant. Zadok and Abiathar, the priests, spoke to the elders of the tribe to win their support. Rebels were forgiven, and Amasa, the leader of the rebel forces, was appointed commander of the army in place of Joab. These acts of conciliation on the part of David insured him a cordial welcome when he returned to take his throne.

Sheba's Rebellion. A second rebellion during David's latter years was that of Sheba, son of Bichri, of the tribe of Benjamin. Complaining that the ten tribes had not been given sufficient honor he summoned them to revolt. Amasa was too late in mustering David's army and Abishai was sent forth with the king's personal bodyguard. Joab, who had never forgotten Amasa's promotion at his expense, met him on the road and slew him. Taking command of the troops, Joab beseiged Sheba in Abel of Beth-maachah. When Sheba's head was thrown down from the wall by a woman of the city, both siege and rebellion were ended.

Famine. After civil war a new form of distress, famine, prevailed throughout the land of Israel. When the reason for the famine was sought from God, an act of Saul in slaying the Gibeonites was mentioned. No record of this is given elsewhere in Scripture. Saul seems to have massacred a group of Gibeonites in order to seize their vineyards.

When the cause of the famine was known, the Gibeonites were asked to determine the remedy. In accord with the common Semitic concept of blood revenge they asked that seven lives from among the Israelites be given. Seven men were hanged at Gibeah, after which the famine was ended.

Numbering the People. The purpose of a census in antiquity was military conscription or taxation. David decided to "number the people" as a means of ascertaining his strength. The Philistines continued to be restive; it would seem the path of wisdom to be prepared for attack. The deed, however, was interpreted as an insult to Israel's God, who could save by few or by many.

The prophet Gad brought to David a choice of one of three possible chastisements: seven years of famine; three months of defeat in battle; three days of pestilence. Choosing to fall into the hands of the Lord rather than of man, David chose the pestilence. In the midst of the severe pestilence David acknowledged the enormity of his sin. When a destroying angel was approaching Jerusalem, David was directed to meet him on Mount Moriah at the threshing floor of Araunah the Jebusite. There a sacrifice was offered and God's wrath was appeased. The site of Araunah's threshing floor later became the Temple mount.

David's Last Days. David's last days were marked by physical weakness and a contest among his sons for the throne which they knew would soon be relinquished. David did live long enough to designate Solomon as his heir and give him counsel concerning the way in which he should rule. After his forty-year reign, David was buried on Mount Zion, ending one of the most memorable periods of Israel's history.

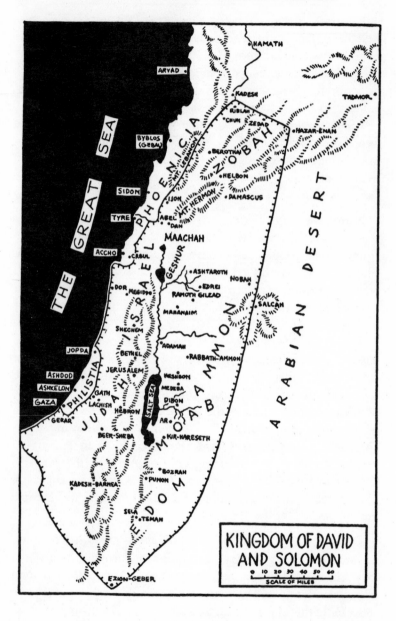

CHAPTER 12

SOLOMON: ISRAEL'S GOLDEN AGE

UNDER SOLOMON, Israel reached the period of its greatest outward splendor. Under him it also began its period of decadence. A son of David's more mature years, he knew nothing of the early struggles of David's life. Solomon ruled in splendor befitting an oriental potentate and in so doing hastened the division and ultimately the downfall of Israel as a political entity.

Accession of Solomon. In the declining years of David a controversy developed between rival claimants to the throne. Adonijah, David's oldest living son, was considered heir-apparent. Joab, David's commander, and Abiathar the priest supported his claims. Plans were made for a public festival in

which Adonijah's right to the throne would be proclaimed
when word reached Nathan, the prophet.

Nathan informed Bathsheba of Adonijah's ambitions. She,
as Solomon's mother, had ambitions of her own. Supported by
Nathan and Zadok, the priest, she reminded David of an earlier
promise that Solomon would be the royal heir.

David acquiesced in the request of Bathsheba, and ordered the
formal anointing of Solomon. Cherethites and Pelethites, foreign mercenaries serving as David's personal bodyguards, were
on hand to intervene in the event of violence.

The plans of Bathsheba and Nathan were carried out without incident. Near the spring Gihon, Zadok anointed Solomon
as king. The assembled multitude shouted, "Long live King
Solomon!" The shout was heard at En-rogel, where Adonijah
and his partisans were gathered. Puzzled at the unexpected
commotion, Joab asked the reason for the uproar. A messenger
brought word that David had made Solomon king.

Adonijah's partisans were caught off guard. The company
quickly dispersed, and Adonijah sought asylum at the horns of
the altar and pleaded that his life be spared. Solomon assured
him that he would be safe if he were not guilty of subsequent
misconduct.

Until the death of David, Solomon took no action to remove
potential enemies or rivals. After David's death a veritable
purge took place in which Adonijah and his most conspicuous
partisans were successively removed.

Adonijah made the mistake of requesting permission to marry Abishag, the Shunammite companion of David's old age. The
records do not state that David had married Abishag, but
Solomon's reaction to Adonijah's request indicates that he regarded it as a hidden claim to the throne. Marriage to a king's
widow brought with it political implications. Rightly or wrong-
ly, Solomon put this construction on the request and ordered the
death of Adonijah.

The priest Abiathar, who had supported Adonijah, was deposed and the valiant Joab, who had served as David's commander for many years, was killed by Benaiah, a partisan of

Solomon. Thus Solomon was left to organize his kingdom without fear of opposition.

Early Years. The beginning of Solomon's reign was one of peace and prosperity. Tribute was coming to Jerusalem from the Aramaeans, the Ammonites, the Moabites, the Philistines and the Edomites. Jerusalem was fast becoming a cosmopolitan city, and its king gained a reputation for wisdom which was regarded as the special gift he had chosen from God rather than fame or worldly success. This wisdom enabled him to decide difficult legal matters. Solomon also became famous as a solver of riddles, a speaker of proverbs and a student of nature.

Marriage. Solomon is known both for his wisdom and for his enormous harem of one thousand wives and concubines. There can be no doubt that his harem was motivated both by a desire for grandeur and political considerations. His marriage with a daughter of the Egyptian Pharaoh is indicative of the place of Israel in international affairs. For centuries Israel had held at least nominal control over Palestine, but now Solomon was treated as an equal by foreign monarchs.

The city of Gezer, an ancient Canaanite stronghold which guards a pass from the region of Jaffa to Jerusalem, was given by the Pharaoh to Solomon as a wedding present. This is another reminder of the slow process by which the land of Canaan came under Israelite control.

Building the Temple. David had not been permitted to build the Temple in Jerusalem, but he was told that it would be built by his son. Solomon's energies were expended in the building of the Temple. Tribute from subject peoples, materials and craftsmen from Tyre and Lebanon made possible a building which defies description. The Sanctuary itself, including the floor and the walls, was covered with pure gold. Besides the Sanctuary with its Holy Place where the priests ministered and the Holy of Holies which was entered once a year on the Day of Atonement by the high priest, there were porches, chapels and courts. In the Court of the Priests, daily sacrifices were offered. The dedication of the Temple was a high spot in the life of Solomon. He humbly acknowledged his dependence upon the God of Israel and pledged his loyalty to Him.

Other Building Operations.   Although the Temple was the best known of Solomon's building operations, others of a more secular nature would likewise give him a claim to fame. The city of Megiddo, excavated by the University of Chicago, still contains the ruins of stables built for Solomon's chariotry. Other chariotry installations were located at Jerusalem, Hazor and Gezer (I Kings 4:26; 9:15-19).

With the aid of Phoenician technicians, Solomon built the seaport of Ezion-geber at the head of the Gulf of Aqaba. A copper refinery was built nearby, indicating that some of Solomon's wealth came from the export of copper. Nelson Glueck discovered the ruins of Solomon's refinery during excavations of *Tell el-Kheleifeh,* ancient Ezion-geber, during the years 1938-40.

In the wilderness east of Damascus, Solomon built (or rebuilt) the city of Tadmor, known since Roman times as Palmyra. It served as a caravan center where merchants from Syria and the Euphrates region might trade with those from Egypt and other lands to the south. In the time of the Romans, Palmyra was a stopping place for caravans traveling from India to Rome.

Another city better known for its Roman ruins than for those of the Solomonic era is Baalbeck, or Baalath. Before the time of Solomon there is no suggestion that the Israelites gave attention to architecture and building operations. Their most ornate structure, the Tabernacle, was a tent built with costly materials to serve as a portable sanctuary. With Solomon, however, Israel gave attention to the cultural elements of architecture and literature as well as the necessities of defense and self-preservation.

International relations. Hiram of Tyre was of great help in Solomon's building programs, and a marriage-alliance with Egypt stood him in good stead with the Pharoahs. Solomon imported horses, chariots and linen yarn from Egypt (I Kings 10: 28, 29). From Ophir and Tarshish, ships brought gold, silver, ivory, apes, peacocks (or "baboons," according to another translation) and algum-wood. The nature of the products and the length of time involved in the voyage (three years) suggest India, or some land having access to India, as the land where Ophir was located. Tarshish was probably in Spain.

The visit of the Queen of Sheba to Solomon probably came as a result of contacts made by Solomon's traders with the Sabaean kingdom in the southern part of Arabia. She brought with her camels bearing spices, gold and precious stones. In addition to satisfying her curiosity concerning Solomon, she doubtless made trade arrangements on behalf of her people.

Solomon's Defection. The success of Solomon in international affairs had a price tag attached to it. Jerusalem became a truly cosmopolitan city with both foreign wives in the king's harem and foreign merchants plying their wares. These wives, in particular, had to be treated as would befit royalty. They brought with them the worship of the gods of their homelands.

Solomon built shrines, or high places, for these gods. He not only made provision for his wives to worship their local gods, but he was led into idolatry himself. It is tragic to observe the king who was noted for his wisdom entering a period of weakness and moral bankruptcy.

The Kingdom Begins to Disintegrate. During the latter days of Solomon's reign the subject peoples were able to assert their independence. Rezon reigned over the Damascus area as an avowed enemy of Solomon. Hadad returned from exile in Egypt to claim his territory in Edom. A prophet named Ahijah declared to Jeroboam the son of Nebat that he would rule ten of the tribes because of the idolatry of Solomon's rule. When Solomon attempted to kill Jeroboam he fled to Egypt to find asylum there. Friendly relations between Egypt and Solomon seem to have ended. The burden of taxation at home, the falling away of the subject provinces and the religious apostasy of Solomon's latter days bequeathed to his successor problems which defied solution.

Solomon's Death. After a forty-year reign the king who is esteemed the wisest of men died, leaving his country on the verge of bankruptcy. He had wonderful opportunities and wonderful accomplishments, but his defection tended to nullify much of his good beginning.

CHAPTER 13

JEROBOAM SPLITS THE KINGDOM AND RULES THE NORTH

The Disruption. During the latter part of Solomon's reign much dissatisfaction prevailed because of the heavy taxation and forced labor projects needed to maintain the splendor of the court. This dissatisfaction came to a head when Rehoboam succeeded to the throne after Solomon's death.

The tribe of Ephraim was the center of disaffection. The north had a tradition of independence never wholly surrendered. Ephraim, in particular, looked upon itself as a sovereign tribe. Concessions were demanded of Rehoboam before he would be recognized as king. This was no new procedure. After the death of Saul, his son Esh-baal was recognized as king in the north while David ruled in the south. During the reign of David there had been two contests for the throne, one of which (that of Sheba) had a strong appeal to the northern tribes.

81

The city of Shechem, Ephraim's principal city, was chosen for the coronation of Rehoboam. The leaders of the tribes saw in the event an opportunity to petition the heir apparent to relax the tax burden imposed by Solomon. Rehoboam scornfully refused, insisting that he would tax the people more heavily than his father had done. Thereupon the northern tribes renounced loyalty to the house of David and Rehoboam barely escaped with his life.

Jeroboam I (the Son of Nebat.)   Jeroboam, the leader of the revolt had served as an administrative officer under Solomon. When Solomon learned of the prophecy that he would become ruler of ten of the tribes, he tried to kill Jeroboam. Jeroboam, however, escaped to Egypt where he was protected by Pharaoh Shishak. On hearing news of Solomon's death, Jeroboam returned to Shechem. He headed the deputation which asked concessions of Rehoboam, and when Rehoboam refused to grant them, Jeroboam encouraged the northern tribes to rebel.

When the northern tribes determined to disown the rule of Rehoboam they turned to Jeroboam for leadership. The tribe of Judah, with the chief part of Benjamin, and probably some from Dan, Simeon and other tribes, acknowledged Rehoboam as king. Jeroboam, however, ruled the largest and best portion of the land. The division of the kingdom took place about 930 B.C.

The Golden Calves.   Jeroboam determined to make his northern tribes self-sufficient. In order to prevent the people from going to Jerusalem at the time of the great festivals he established sanctuaries, with golden calves, at Bethel and at Dan. Probably Jeroboam did not mean to imply that the God of Israel was a bull-god. Israel's neighbors, Canaanites, Aramaeans and Hittites, commonly represented their deities as sitting or standing on the back of an animal. In similar fashion, Jeroboam may have simply desired to picture the Lord as enthroned on golden calves. The tendency, however, was to idolatry, and the Biblical writers constantly speak of the calves as abominations. Jeroboam went down in history as the king "who made Israel to sin."

Shishak's Invasion. Shishak, or Sheshonk, was the founder of the Twenty-second Dynasty, a line of Lybian kings who ruled Egypt for two centuries. The division of the kingdom of Israel and the civil war which followed made both north and south an easy prey for an aggressive conqueror. Shishak dreamed of restoring Egypt to the position it enjoyed under Thothmes III. He invaded both Judah and Israel during the reigns of Rehoboam and Jeroboam, recording an account of his victories on a temple pylon at Karnak. Over one hundred towns are listed as conquered by Shishak's armies. His earlier friendship for Jeroboam did not prevent him from attacking cities of the Northern Kingdom.

Shishak's gold-masked body was found intact in his burial chamber at Tanis during an expedition there in the 1938-39 season. He was not one of Egypt's great rulers, although he might have controlled all of Palestine had he followed up his advantage there.

Building Projects. Jeroboam realized early in his career the need for adequate protection. Judah could be expected to dispute his claim to sovereignty over the north, hence adequate defensive measures had to be taken.

Jeroboam built, or fortified, Shechem, and built his palace at nearby Tirzah. Tirzah was a place of beauty, commemorated with Jerusalem in the Song of Solomon (6:4). The kings of Israel made Tirzah their home until the days of Omri, the builder of Samaria.

East of the Jordan, Jeroboam built fortifications at Peniel on the Jabbok, the place where Jacob had wrestled with the angel. Fortifications were not successful in bringing victory to the arms of Jeroboam, however. Battles with Judah, the Southern Kingdom, resulted in a virtual stalemate, and losses to Egypt were great.

Nadab. Jeroboam died after a reign of twenty-two years, leaving the crown to Nadab, his son. Nothing significant is recorded of Nadab. He followed the evil example of his father and, after a reign of only two years, while he was besieging a Philistine town, he was murdered by Baasha, a man of Issachar.

The Problem of Dynasty. Throughout its history the Southern Kingdom (Judah) had only one dynasty, that of King David. In the North, however, there were nine dynasties with nineteen kings. Plots against the reigning king, with the murder and massacre of his relatives, became common. When his son Nadab was murdered, the dynasty of Jeroboam came to an end.

TOPICS

CHAPTER 14

ISRAEL: BAASHA TO THE DYNASTY OF OMRI

Baasha. The murderer of Nadab destroyed all of the house of Jeroboam to insure an unquestioned right to the throne. He then proceeded to fortify Ramah, the home of the prophet Samuel, which was located only five miles from Jerusalem. Ramah was strategically situated near an important pass so that it could serve both defensive and offensive purposes.

The Aramaeans. To meet this dangerous threat to Judah, Asa, king of the Southern Kingdom, sent heavy tribute to Ben-hadad, king of the Aramaean state of Damascus. Damascus and its environs had been subdued by David, but Rezon, a servant of Hadadezer, king of the neighboring state of Zobah, had seized Damascus and opposed Solomon. The loss of tribute from Damascus may have been one of the reasons why such heavy taxes were imposed on Israel by Solomon and Rehoboam.

By the time of Ben-hadad, Damascus had become a powerful state, ready to take any means to extend its borders. Ben-hadad eased the pressure on Jerusalem by attacking northern Israel. Baasha gave up his plans to fortify Ramah and rushed to the defense of his northern borders. The forces of Ben-hadad laid waste the towns of Ijon, Dan and Abel-beth-maachah, with the district around the Lake of Galilee and the tribe of Naphtali.

By forcing Israel to fight on two fronts, Judah had achieved an immediate victory. Ultimately, however, the kingdom of Damascus would prove a threat to the Southern Kingdom as well as to that of the North.

Elah.   After a reign of twenty-four years, Baasha left the kingdom to his son Elah, who reigned over Israel two years. Elah suffered the same fate at the hands of Zimri, one of his captains, that Nadab suffered at the hands of Baasha. In each case an energetic leader seized the kingdom, ruled effectively for more than two decades, and left the kingdom to a weak son who was unable to defend either the kingdom or himself.

Zimri.   Zimri put an end to the second dynasty of Israel, but he reigned only one week. Omri, another claimant to the throne, besieged Zimri in the royal palace at Tirzah. In desperation, Zimri set fire to the palace and perished in the flames.

Omri.   For four years Omri and Tibni contested the crown of Israel. When Omri emerged victorious, he built a new palace on the hill of Samaria instead of rebuilding the one destroyed by Zimri at Tirzah. From this time on Samaria served as the capital of the Northern Kingdom. Prophets spoke of the judgments of God on the North under the terms of Samaria (its capital), Ephraim (its principal tribe) or Israel.

In the Assyrian monuments, Israel is known as "Beth-Omri," the house of Omri. This is a tribute to the importance of Omri from their viewpoint. Although his Biblical importance is overshadowed by that of his infamous son, Ahab, Omri was a vigorous ruler.

Omri sought to establish diplomatic relations with the Phoenicians and thus arranged for the marriage of his son, Ahab, with Jezebel, daughter of Ethbaal, king of Sidon (I Kings 18: 18). The political advantage may have been great, but this union later produced fearful results both in Israel and in Judah.

The "Moabite Stone," set up by Mesha, king of Moab, at Dibon, north of the Arnon, tells how Omri gained control of northern Moab, occupying its cities and extracting heavy tribute. Omri does not appear to have had to defend himself against the Aramaeans of Damascus, however, because of the growing power of Assyria. Ben-hadad, along with the other petty kings of the city-states of Syria and Palestine, looked with anxiety on the growth of the nation which would one day rule the entire territory to the Medtierranean except for a small area around Jerusalem.

Ahab and Jezebel. After a reign of twelve years, Omri was succeeded by his son Ahab, known for his encouragement of Baal-worship in Israel. Jeroboam had introduced "golden calves" which served as snares in the way of the true worship of the God of Israel. Ahab, however, abetted by his Phoenician wife, —Jezebel, promoted the worship of the Tyrian Baal as the god of the land. An altar and a temple to Baal were erected in Samaria, and attempts were made to suppress the worship of the Lord.

Elijah. The man who singlehandedly challenged Ahab and Jezebel was the prophet Elijah. Prophesying drought throughout the land, he struck terror into the heart of the idolatrous king. Supernaturally preserved by God during the time of famine, Elijah uttered his famous challenge to Ahab, asking him to bring together the priests of Baal at Mount Carmel in order to determine who should be recognized as God of Israel. Only Elijah's God answered "by fire" when sacrifices were provided, and the priests of Baal were slain. Subsequently the drought was ended. It is significant that Baal was regarded as a fertility god . The God of Elijah was in control of the rains as well as Lord of all creation.

Ahab and Ben-hadad. Late in the reign of Ahab, Ben-hadad of Damascus, with a coalition of thirty-two vassals, invaded Israel from the north, reaching the gates of Samaria. Ahab's brilliant strategy won the battle for Samaria (I Kings 20). Rationalizing that the "gods of Israel" were gods of the hills, Ben-hadad determined to fight on the plains the following year. At Aphek, east of the Sea of Galilee, on the road from Damascus to Bethshan, a battle was fought a year later with even more disastrous results for the Syrians. Ben-hadad humbled himself before Ahab who spared his life and made a league with him.

The Battle of Karkar. Shalmaneser III (859-824 B.C.) directed the Assyrian armies southwestward toward Syria and Palestine, intent on adding them to his subject peoples. In 853 B.C. a coalition of states headed by "Hadadezer [Ben-hadad] of Aram [Damascus]" challenged the Assyrian invaders at Karkar, north of Hamath, on the Orontes River.

The monolith inscription of Shalmaneser III, now in the British Museum states that "Ahab, the Israelite" provided two thousand chariots, as compared with twelve hundred from Hadadezer. Ahab also is reported to have provided ten thousand soldiers as compared with twenty thousand from Damascus.

Although Shalmaneser claimed a great victory at Karkar, the facts indicate otherwise. Karkar guarded the approach to lower Syria, but Shalmaneser did not move south to Hamath as he would be expected to do in the event of victory. After Karkar, some years passed before Damascus was again attacked, indicating that the battle was certainly not a decisive one.

Death of Ahab. War between Ben-hadad and Ahab was renewed with a campaign in Ramoth in Gilead, east of the Jordan.

Jehoshaphat of Judah joined Ahab in the battle with the Syrians at Ramoth-gilead. Warning from a faithful prophet, Micaiah, was unheeded. The kings entered the battle only to be defeated. Ahab was slain, his army disbanded and Jehoshaphat barely escaped. Ben-hadad gained control of the Israelite territory west of the Jordan.

Ahaziah. After Ahab's twenty-two-year reign his son Ahaziah took the throne, reigning only two years. Ahaziah was a less forceful character than his father, but he followed Ahab's idolatrous ways. Elijah remonstrated with him for seeking information from Baal-zebub, the god of Ekron (probably originally "Baal-zeboul," meaning "Baal-exalted," intentionally perverted by the Israelites into "Baal-zebub," "lord of flies").

The Moabites, subject to Israel during the days of Omri and Ahab, rebelled early in the reign of Ahaziah. Mesha of Moab drove the Israelite garrisons from the land and made himself master of the entire territory. The "Moabite Stone" is his record of this victory over the Israelites.

Jehoram. After the brief reign of Ahaziah (two years) he was succeeded by his brother Jehoram, or Joram. Twice during the twelve-year reign of Jehoram the Assyrians attacked Syria, but there is no record of Israelite participation in the defense of her neighbor to the north. Ahab's death at the hands of Ben-hadad at Ramoth-gilead doubtless acted as a deterrent to his sons when it came to joining further alliances against Assyria.

Elisha Succeeds Elijah. Normally there is no principle of succession in the prophetic ministry, but Elisha forms an exception. At the time of Elijah's impressive ascent heavenward, the mantle of the prophet who had resisted Baalism fell upon Elisha. Both Elijah and Elisha stood out as prophets of the Lord in a period of idolatry. Miracles are recorded in connection with the ministry of each. God did not leave Himself without a witness.

Wars with Syria. Elisha appears as a patriot as well as a prophet in the wars with Syria during the reign of Jehoram. Ben-hadad inquired concerning recovery from sickness during a visit of Elisha to Damascus. The prophet assured the king that the disease was not fatal, but Ben-hadad was near his end. The next day an officer of Ben-hadad, Hazael, suffocated his master and usurped the throne.

In a new battle between Syria and Israel at Ramoth-gilead Jehoram was wounded. He retired to Jezreel where his cousin, King Ahaziah of Judah, came to see him. In the meantime Jehu, a captain of Jehoram's, was conducting the campaign at Ramoth-gilead when one of the "sons of the prophets" anointed him king of Israel and commissioned him to destroy the wicked house of Ahab.

Acknowledged as king by the army, Jehu crossed the Jordan and headed toward Jezreel. When Jehoram rode forth to meet the usurper he was struck down by an arrow from Jehu's hand. Ahaziah of Judah was mortally wounded as he fled toward Megiddo. Jezebel was flung down from a window in Jezreel and devoured by dogs. Seventy sons of Ahab were killed in Samaria along with the priests and worshipers of Baal who were enticed into the Baal temple, and then killed to a man. Thus Jehu extirpated Baalism from Israel, but at tremendous cost in blood and ill will.

CHAPTER 15

THE DYNASTY OF JEHU

JEHU. Jehu's purge of Baalism created serious political problems. The Phoenicians were friendly to the dynasty of Omri, and the murder of Jezebel, a Phoenician princess, could only mean hatred from that direction. Athaliah of Judah, a daughter of Ahab and Jezebel and a Baal-worshiper could be counted upon to oppose the policies of Jehu.

A black obelisk found in 1845 at Nimrud (Biblical Calah on the Tigris) gives us a supplementary note on the foreign policy of Jehu. Shalmaneser III, who had fought a coalition of Syrian states, including Israel, at Karkar, during the time of Ahab, is depicted as receiving tribute from Jehu. Either Jehu or one of his emissaries is pictured kissing the ground at the feet of Shalmaneser and offering as tribute, bars and vessels of gold, silver, and lead. Underneath this picture is the inscription: "Tribute of Jehu the son of Omri." Evidently Jehu felt it the part of wisdom to pay his tribute quietly to the Assyrians.

In his annals, Shalmaneser mentions a campaign in the twenty-first year of his reign in which he conquered four of the towns subject to Hazael of Damascus. The absence of any reference to Israel indicates that, although forced to pay tribute, Israel's borders were secure against invasion from Assyria.

Jehu's willingness to co-operate with Assyria quite naturally incurred the wrath of Hazael. As Shalmaneser was compelled to abandon his Syrian campaigns because of other pressing concerns, Hazael turned toward the eastern domains of Israel as legitimate plunder. When Gilead and Bashan fell into the hands of Hazael, Jehu doubtless had occasion to question his policies.

In spite of Jehu's zeal for the Lord and opposition to Baalism, the verdict of Scripture is that he "departed not from the sins of Jeroboam which made Israel to sin" (II Kings 10:31). At a later time Hosea prophesied, "For yet a little while and I will avenge the blood of Jezreel upon the house of Jehu, and will cause to cease the kingdom of the house of Israel" (Hosea 1:4).

Jehoahaz.   Jehu's twenty-eight-year reign was the longest of any of the kings of Israel since the division of the kingdom. When the heir, Jehoahaz, came to the throne, Hazael continued his attacks, reducing Israel to a subject status. Rigid military restrictions were placed on Israel and its territory included little more than the hill-country of Ephraim. Aramaean armies passed through Israel at will and actually occupied the Philistine plain from which Jerusalem was threatened.

Under Adad-nirari III, Assyria attacked Hazael who was forced to surrender and pay high tribute. During the siege of Damascus delegates arrived from Tyre, Sidom, Edom, Philistia and *Bit Humria* ("House of Omri" or Israel) with tribute for the Assyrian king.

The power of Hazael was not completely broken by the Assyrians, however. Within four years Hazael proceeded against the Philistines, oppressing Judah along the way as mentioned above. Yet the period of Damascus' power was over. Israel regained her boundaries and enjoyed a time of relative independence until the Assyrians struck their death blow.

Joash. After a seventeen-year reign, Jehoahaz died, leaving his throne to his son Joash. During the reign of Jehoram Ben-hadad I, son of Hazael, had besieged Samaria and brought about such fearful conditions that mothers are said to have killed and eaten their own babies. As prophesied by Elisha, panic broke out in the camp of the Aramaeans and they suddenly withdrew. Shortly before his death, Elisha assured Joash of victory over the Aramaeans. When an attack by Ben-hadad against Zakir of Hamath ended in a draw, Joash attacked Syria and regained the cities of Israel which had been lost during the reign of Jehoahaz (II Kings 13:25).

During the last years of his reign, Joash attacked Amaziah of Judah, near Beth-shemesh. Amaziah was taken captive, Jerusalem was plundered and Temple and palace treasures were taken by the armies of Israel. About 250 yards of the wall of Jerusalem were demolished and hostages were demanded to guarantee the preservation of peace. The Southern Kingdom was thus rendered subject to the kingdom of Israel.

Jeroboam II. Jeroboam II, the son of Joash, came to the throne during a notable period of Israelite expansion. He continued to regain land lost to the Syrians in northern Israel and in the country east of the Jordan (Gilead and Bashan). Even Moab was rendered tributary for a time. Assyria had a succession of weak rulers (Shalmaneser IV, Ashur-dan III and Ash-ur-nirari V) who did not endanger the West.

The rule of Jeroboam II was a kind of Indian summer in Israel's history. With territory extending "from the entrance of Hamath to the sea of the plains," a period of unparalleled prosperity was enjoyed. Yet during this period of peace and prosperity, the prophets Amos and Hosea appeared on the horizon predicting imminent judgment. The wealthy lived lives of ease, feasting in their ivory-decorated houses while the poor were oppressed. Sacrifices were presented to the Lord, but they were mere rituals. Amos and Hosea both prophesied that Israel would be taken into captivity.

Zachariah. After a reign of forty-one years, the longest of the reigns of the kings of Israel, Jeroboam II died, passing on the kingdom to his son Zachariah. Within six months, Zachariah was murdered by a usurper, Shallum, whose one-month reign began a period of decline which ended with the capture of Samaria by the Assyrians.

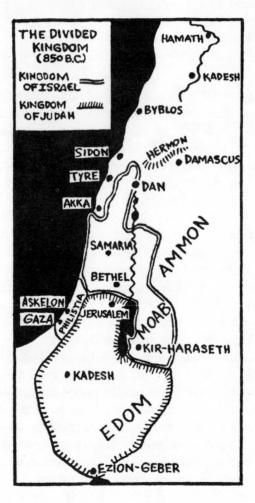

CHAPTER 16

DECLINE AND DEFEAT OF THE NORTHERN KINGDOM

A STATE OF ANARCHY followed the death of Jeroboam II. Politically the people were divided into parties favorable to Damascus, Assyria and Egypt. Regicide followed regicide so that only one king after Jeroboam II died a natural death.

Shallum. Zachariah had reigned six months when he was murdered by Shallum, a partisan of the group which favored friendship and alliance with Damascus. Shallum had reigned one month when he was murdered by Menahem.

Menahem. About the time of the death of Jeroboam II, a usurper who took the name of Tiglath-pileser III seized the

throne of Assyria. He was also known as Pulu, and is called
Pul in the Bible (II Kings 15:19).

Tiglath-pileser successfully attacked Armenia and several
provinces in upper Syria. Rezin of Damascus, Menahem of Israel and an Arabian queen paid obeisance to him. Menahem
paid tribute of one thousand talents of silver by imposing a levy
of fifty shekels upon every Israelite able to pay.

Pekahiah. After a reign of ten years, Menahem was succeeded by his son Pekahiah who was murdered by one of his
captains, Pekah, after ruling only two years.

Pekah. Pekah belonged to the party which felt that an alliance with Damascus was the best means of avoiding destruction by Assyria. Rezin of Damascus and Pekah of Israel formed
an alliance against Tiglath-pileser. Philistia and Edom, under
pressure from Israel and Syria, joined the alliance. Ahaz of
Judah, however, refused to join. To cripple Judah as an effective
opponent or to force her to join the alliance, Rezin and Pekah
invaded the Southern Kingdom and besieged Jerusalem. It was
under these circumstances that Isaiah assured Ahaz that Jerusalem would be spared. Ahaz, however, sent tribute to Tiglath-
pileser with a request for aid. When Rezin and Pekah learned
that Tiglath-pileser was preparing to march against Syria-Pales-
tine they abandoned the siege of Jersualem.

Tiglath-pileser proceeded to overrun northern Israel, taking
"Ijon and Abel-beth-maacha, and Janoah, and Kedesh, and
Hazor, and Gilead, and Galilee, all the land of Naphtali . . ."
(II Kings 15:29), and deporting their inhabitants to Assyria.

The Fall of Damascus. Having ravaged the land of Israel,
Tiglath-pileser turned against Damascus, which he succeeded in
conquering after a long siege. Assyrian records claim the capture of 591 towns of the "sixteen districts of Aram." Rezin was
put to death, ending for all time the Aramaean Kingdom of
Damascus (732 B.C.).

Hoshea. After a period of ten years of tumult and anarchy under Pekah, Hoshea established himself as the last king of Israel. By this time the kingdom had shrunk to the hills of Ephraim, with an Assyrian province to the north and an Assyrian vassal to the south. As long as Hoshea paid tribute to Assyria he was permitted to reign unmolested. When Shalmaneser V came to the Assyrian throne, Hoshea, influenced by the anti-Assyrian party, withheld payment of tribute. In 725 B.C. when Shalmaneser undertook a campaign against him, Hoshea paid his tribute. In 724 B.C., backed by the Egyptian Pharaoh So, Hoshea risked another refusal. The Assyrians marched against him and he was captured at the beginning of the hostilities. He may have actually surrendered himself, asking for mercy. Samaria finally capitulated after a three-year siege during which Shalmaneser had died and his brother Sargon II had become king.

The End of the Northern Kingdom. Sargon adopted the policy of transportation first used by Tiglath-pileser in dealing with captive peoples. Israelites were carried into Assyria and assigned lands where the local inhabitants had likewise been transferred to other countries. People uprooted and resettled in a foreign environment were considered less likely to rebel. Some Israelites were settled in the province of Halah in Mesopotamia; others were located in Media.

With the deportation of Israelites from their homeland the history of the ten tribes comes to an end. Apart from a few scattered remnants whose history continues with that of Judah, the people of the Northern Kingdom vanished from history.

The thought that these so-called "lost tribes" are hidden somewhere and will reappear at the end of history is unwarranted. They were neither destroyed nor did they migrate to some distant land. Like most of the other peoples of the ancient world (e.g., Moabites, Ammonites, Jebusites, Hittites, Amorites, etc.) they were assimilated into their new environment. Their distinctive Israelite culture and religion were lost in their mingling with the people among whom they settled. In the case

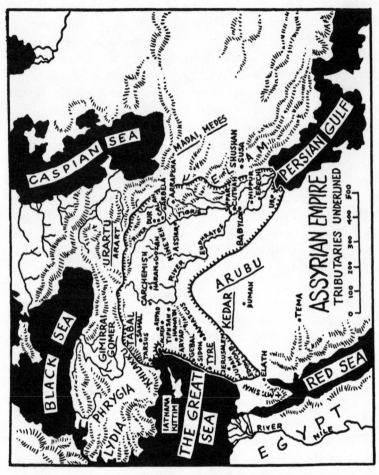

At its greatest extent the Assyrian Empire also included Egypt.

of the Northern Kingdom, idolatry not only brought the end to the political state, but it also brought an end to the history of a people. We shall have occasion to note that the Southern Kingdom, Judah, likewise suffered political catastrophe. Faith in the Lord, however, bound the people together until they could return to their land.

The Samaritans. Sargon and his successors, Esarhaddon and Ashurbanipal, repopulated the region of Samaria with colonists from various places—"Babylon, Cuthah, Avva, Hamath, Sepharvaim" (II Kings 17:24). Sargon himself, in a cylinder inscription, lists numerous north Arabian tribes which he settled in "Bit-Humria" doubtless the first Arabs settled in Palestine proper.

In the depopulated condition of Samaria, wild animals began to appear in alarming numbers. These were regarded as a punishment from "the god of the land" who was not receiving his due worship. The new inhabitants had brought their own gods, but they had evidently neglected "the god of the land." Thus Sargon ordered one of the deported priests to return and teach the people the proper means of worshiping the Lord and to constitute priests who would perform the requisite acts.

The Samaritans, as the new population of Samaria came to be called, were a mixed people. They contained the remnants of the Israelites whom the Assyrian kings did not deport, with the newcomers who felt it necessary to worship "the god of the land" along with their other gods. Gradually the worship of the Lord became the exclusive religion of the Samaritans, although they continued to be looked upon with suspicion by the orthodox Judeans of the Southern Kingdom. Nehemiah refused to co-operate with the Samaritans and the antipathy between the two peoples is apparent throughout the gospel records.

TOPICS

Rehoboam	Ahaziah
Abijam	Athaliah
Asa	Joash
Jehoshaphat	Amaziah
Jehoram	Uzziah

CHAPTER 17

JUDAH: FROM REHOBOAM TO UZZIAH

THE KINGDOM OF JUDAH, or the Southern Kingdom, had a history of about four centuries after the death of Solomon and the division of the country. Its nineteen kings were all lineal descendants of King David.

Rehoboam. After his rejection by the northern tribes at Shechem, Rehoboam mustered an army and sought to bring the entire nation under his control. Through the intervention of Shemaiah, the prophet, Rehoboam's campaign was stopped. He did prepare for war, however, by erecting fortresses and placing garrisons in at least fifteen cities throughout the two tribes which he ruled.

Priests and Levites from the Northern Kingdom came into Judah and added their support to the cause of Rehoboam. The policy of Jeroboam was such that the spiritual leaders were unable to co-operate with him. They would certainly protest the erection of "golden calves" at Bethel and Dan, and they would also wish to go to Jerusalem for the observation of the great stated convocations prescribed in the Mosaic Law. When Jeroboam found the priests and Levites unco-operative he removed them from office and appointed religious leaders who would be responsive to his will.

When the Egyptian Pharaoh, Shishak, marched against Rehoboam, the fortified cities of Judah were rendered useless and Jerusalem itself was despoiled of both palace and Temple treasures. The national calamity brought a sense of sin to the king and people of Judah, so that spiritual good came from it.

Abijam (Abijah).   After a reign of seventeen years, Rehoboam was succeeded by his son Abijam. War with Jeroboam continued. Abijam succeeded in recovering some of the border cities from Israel and in making an alliance with Tab-rimmon of Damascus which forced Jeroboam to give attention to his northern boundaries. Abijam's reign was one of religious apostasy, however. Cult images of various types were venerated and worship at the "high places" involving ritual prostitution was practiced.

Asa.   Abijam's three-year reign may be contrasted with the forty-one years that his son Asa ruled over Judah. Asa began his reign as a reformer who destroyed the cult objects used in Baal worship and sought to bring his people back to a position of loyalty to the Lord and His Law.

Zerah, a Cushite prince (identified with Osorkon I of the Libyan Dynasty of Pharaohs, called a Cushite because of his residence in Upper Egypt), attacked Asa with soldiers and chariots. The army of Asa met Zerah and his troops at Mareshah, in the Valley of Zephathah. Zerah was defeated and the victorious Asa pursued him as far as Gerar.

War with Baasha of Israel was not as successful, however. Asa lost the territory won by Abijam. Baasha was about to fortify Ramah in order to block the kingdom of Judah from the north when Asa appealed to Ben-hadad of Damascus for help. An attack by Ben-hadad on Israel's northern border relieved the pressure on Judah.

Asa's latter days saw a relapse from his earlier faith. Hanani, a prophet, upbraided him for lack of faith in making a covenant with Ben-hadad and was cast into prison for such impertinence. Suffering from a serious foot disease during the last three years of his life, Asa was forced to turn the government over to his son, Jehoshaphat. Asa is said to have "sought not to the Lord but to the physicians" in his sickness, and it may be suspected that the king's faithlessness encouraged the people to lapse again into idolatry.

Jehoshaphat. Jehoshaphat was a contemporary of Ahab, Ahaziah and Jehoram, kings of Israel. His godly life stands in marked contrast to theirs, however.

Jehoshaphat was able to keep the Philistines and Arabians under tribute. He joined forces with Ahab in fighting the Syrians at Ramoth-gilead, but narrowly escaped with his life in the battle in which Ahab was killed. He was more successful in an encounter with combined forces from Ammon, Edom and Moab. Before Jehoshaphat came to the field of battle, the three allies quarreled among themselves. Jehoshaphat emerged the victor without striking a blow.

Since Edom was subject to Judah, Jehoshaphat was able to organize a naval expedition directed toward Ophir, probably in southwestern Arabia. Ships were built with the aid of Ahaziah of Israel and the Tyrian king, but they were wrecked before the expedition got under way.

Jehoshaphat sincerely attempted to encourage his people to lives of obedience to the Law of the Lord. Yet he was responsible for an act which brought Baalism into Judah. Early in his reign he attempted to heal the breach between Israel and Judah by marrying the crown prince, Jehoram, to Ahab's daughter, Athaliah. Thus the door was opened to a policy in Judah analogous to that pursued by Ahab and Jezebel in Israel.

Jehoram. The eight-year reign of Jehoram marked a new low in the history of Judah. Dominated by Athaliah, Jehoram built high places to Baal throughout Judah, and even built a Baal-temple in Jerusalem. As a despotic ruler he ordered the assassination of his brothers and of such officials as had exhibited resentment over his religious policies. The prophet Elijah remonstrated with him in vain.

Politically, too, Jehoram was a failure. The Edomites revolted, cutting off Judah's sea-route to Arabia. Philistines attacked from the west, and an Arabian attack from the south plundered the palace and carried off the king's harem. All of the sons of Jehoram except Ahaziah (or Jehoahaz) were killed on the field of battle. The king himself died of a painful intestinal disease at the age of forty.

Ahaziah (of Judah). The influence of Athaliah, Ahaziah's mother, dominated the few months of his reign. He actively promoted Baal worship, allying himself with Jehoram of Israel, his mother's brother, in a fresh attempt to wrest Ramoth-gilead from the Aramaeans. The king of Israel was wounded and retired to Jezreel where Ahaziah went to see him. Jehu, soon to be king of Israel, suddenly attacked, killing both Jehoram of Israel and Ahaziah of Judah.

Athaliah. Jehu's massacre of the house of Ahab brought fearful repercussions in the kingdom of Judah. Athaliah, whose son and brother—kings of Judah and Israel, respectively—had been killed at Jezreel, and whose co-religionists were being massacred by Jehu, determined to act. She continued the carnage by destroying her own grandchildren—all the "seed royal" of Judah, with the exception of a single infant who miraculously escaped. For six years she ruled Judah. Resentment smoldered until Jehoiada, the high priest, showed the seven-year-old Joash, the sole remaining heir of David's line, to the captains of the guard. At the proper moment, Joash was presented to the people who shouted, "Long live the king!" In accord with the command of Jehoiada, Athaliah was slain. The temple which had been built to Baal in Jerusalem was destroyed and his priests killed.

Joash. Jehoiada served as guardian for the seven-year-old king, urging him to honor the Lord and His Temple. Under

Athaliah the Temple had deteriorated so that a renovation pro-
gram was badly needed. Gifts and offerings for the purpose
were appropriated and provision was made for an annual collection for the Temple.

Following the death of Jehoiada, Joash lapsed into idolatry.
He had to surrender the Temple treasures to Hazael of Damascus to prevent him from besieging Jerusalem. Resentment
at his policies caused Joash to be murdered in bed by one of his
own servants.

Amaziah. The forty-year reign of Joash was followed by
that of his son, Amaziah, who reigned twenty-nine years, part
of which, Thiele suggests, was a co-regency with Uzziah (Azariah). He prosecuted a war against Edom for the purpose of re-
gaining commercial relations through the port at Ezion-geber.
He victoriously brought home to Jerusalem the gods of Edom
and worshiped them . His attack against Joash of Israel ended in
catastrophe for Amaziah who, some years later, died at the hand
of an assassin.

Uzziah (Azariah). The reign of Uzziah was the longest
yet known in Israel, fifty-two years. He came to the throne at
the age of sixteen and had to put down an Edomite revolt early
in his reign. Although Edom was recognized as independent,
Judah maintained the city of Elath (Ezion-geber) and guarded
the caravan routes to the port.

The reign of Uzziah was one of prosperity, paralleling that
of Jeroboam II in Israel. Walls of Jerusalem were repaired,
cisterns and watchtowers were built, and a high standard of
living was maintained. Ammonites paid tribute, and war was
waged with Philistines and Arabians. Uzziah developed engines
for projecting stones and other missiles in warfare.

Like many another king, the early days of Uzziah's rule were
better than the end. He attempted to assume the functions of
the priests by offering incense in the Temple on the Golden
Altar. Stricken with leprosy, Uzziah spent the last years of his
life in seclusion, his son Jotham acting as regent.

CHAPTER 18

JUDAH DURING THE AGE OF ISAIAH

THE PROPHET ISAIAH received his call to the prophetic ministry during the year of Uzziah's death. He lived during the time when Damascus and Samaria threatened to remove Ahaz from the throne. He saw the fall of the Northern Kingdom and the invasion of Judah by Sennacherib. As a court prophet he maintained close relations to the kings in Jerusalem, with words of rebuke or encouragement as the situation demanded.

Jotham. The sixteen years of Jotham's reign were largely a continuation of the policies of Uzziah. He is credited with numerous building operations—cities, towers and "the high gate of the house of the Lord" (II Chron. 27). He suppressed a revolt of the Ammonites and kept them tributary to Israel.

Isaiah and Micah prophesied during the time of Jotham. They attacked the rich who accumulated vast holdings at the expense of the poor. The distinction between right and wrong was obliterated, and Judah had settled into a complacent type of secularism. Religious festivals were observed and sacrifices were multiplied, but a vital sense of God's presence was missing from the national consciousness.

Toward the close of Jotham's reign, serious threats were made to Judah's independence. Rezin of Damascus and Pekah of

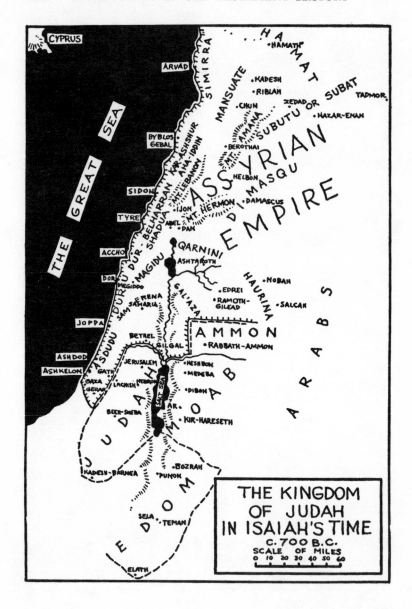

THE KINGDOM
OF JUDAH
IN ISAIAH'S TIME
C. 700 B.C.
SCALE   OF   MILES
0 10 20 30 40 50 60

Israel insisted that Judah join an alliance to offset the impending invasion of Syria and Palestine by Tiglath-pileser III, the most able conqueror and organizer the Assyrians had as yet produced. Jotham refused to join, but the battle that followed this refusal was not fought until after Jotham's death.

Ahaz.   Early in his sixteen-year reign, Ahaz had to deal with the alliance which had been formed by Rezin and Pekah to resist Assyria. Judah was subjected to a series of raids which had as their goal the removal of Ahaz from the throne and the substitution of a ruler more in line with the plans of Rezin and Pekah, Ben-Tabeel by name.

The armies of Judah were unable to cope with the situation. Uzziah had fortified the port of Elath, at the head of the Gulf of Aqabah, and many Judeans had settled there. The forces of Rezin swept past Judah, obtained possession of Elath, expelled the Jewish settlers and restored it to Edom. The traditional text says that Elath was restored to Aram, i.e., Syria. The difference is of one letter in the Hebrew, "d" and "r," which are scarcely distinguishable in manuscript readings. The correct reading appears to be "Edom" (II Kings 16:6).

Edomites and Philistines took advantage of the weakened condition of Israel to engage in marauding expeditions. Philistines actually captured Judean towns and villages, carrying away their inhabitants (II Chron. 28:17 f.).

When the combined forces of Rezin and Pekah approached Jerusalem, Ahaz and his people were terrified. Isaiah gave a message of encouragement and urged confidence in the Lord. He assured Ahaz that both Damascus and Samaria would soon be destroyed. Knowing of Ahaz' plan to invite the aid of the Assyrians, Isaiah warned that momentary relief from Ahaz' problems would bring ultimate ruin. Ahaz, however, refused to heed the prophet's counsel. He asked aid of Tiglath-pileser which the Assyrian was only too glad to give.

Large portions of the northern tribes were annexed to Assyria. Judah was rendered tributary. In 732 B.C. Tiglath-pileser took Damascus and summoned Ahaz and other vassal princes to pay homage to him there. In Damascus, Ahaz saw an impressive heathen altar, a model of which he sent to Urijah the high priest, with instructions to have a copy of it placed in the Temple court.

Religiously Ahaz ranks as one of the most apostate of kings. In addition to the abominations of Baal worship he offered his children to Molech in the Valley of Hinnom.

The last years of Ahaz were difficult indeed. Philistines and Edomites renewed hostilities. Appeals for aid to Tiglath-pileser were met with indifference. Judah was experiencing some of its darkest days.

Hezekiah. Soon after his accession to the throne, Hezekiah carried out a great reformation, assisted no doubt by Isaiah. The high places and cult objects which were contrary to the Mosaic Law were destroyed. The Temple was reopened and a memorable Passover celebrated. Hezekiah strengthened the defenses of Jerusalem, filled the arsenals, and recovered some of the prestige which had been lost during the reign of Ahaz. The Siloam Inscription, found in 1880, describing the construction of a tunnel connecting the Virgin's Spring with the Pool of Siloam may date from this period (cf. II Kings 20:20). Hezekiah encouraged agriculture and we learn from the title of the later collection of Proverbs (25:1) that his scribes were active in the collection and preservation of the literature of the country.

Soon after the accession of Hezekiah, Tiglath-pileser was succeeded by Shalmaneser IV on the throne of Assyria. When Hoshea of Israel refused to pay tribute, Shalmaneser invaded Israel, took Hoshea prisoner, and marched on Samaria. The downfall of the Northern Kingdom must have had a profound effect on thoughtful Judeans.

In the early years of Hezekiah's reign it was apparent that a strong party in Jerusalem advocated an alliance with Egypt against Assyria. Isaiah rejected this policy as strongly as he had rejected the plan of Ahaz to make an alliance with Assyria. His counsel was to trust the Lord.

Either in consequence of Isaiah's ministry or because of external circumstances, Judah did not rebel against Assyria and Jerusalem escaped the fate of Samaria. When Sargon defeated Egypt at the Battle of Raphia, Isaiah's warnings of the futility of reliance on Egypt were vindicated.

In the years when Judah and the neighboring states paid their tribute, Sargon did not concern himself with Palestine. When, as in the case of Ashdod, rebellion took place, Sargon spared no effort in crushing his foes.

With the death of Sargon and the accession of Sennacherib the international picture changed quickly. Merodach-baladan, governor of Babylon, rebelled and he attempted to stir up rebellion in Syria and Palestine. The sickness and recovery of Hezekiah gave Merodach-baladan an excuse for sending an embassy of sympathy and good will to Hezekiah. Actually it turned out to be a political mission. If Merodach could create a "second front" in the west, his revolt in Babylon might succeed. The scheme did not work, however, for Sennacherib conquered Babylon (703 B.C.) and Merodach-baladan fled to Elam where he died.

We do not know what led Hezekiah to rebel in spite of Isaiah's strenuous opposition. Commitments may have been made by his nobles during the time of his illness which he felt obligated to honor. In any event, Assyria quickly intervened. After conquering Babylon and Elam, Sennacherib turned to the Phoenician cities which were in revolt. The king of Sidon escaped, and Tyre was shut up on her island. The Philistine cities fell one by one. Edom and Moab submitted without battle. During the siege of Ekron, news came that Egypt was approaching with an army to contest Sennacherib's power. Sennacherib turned upon his foe and Egypt was defeated at Eltekeh. The hopes of Hezekiah and all who trusted the "broken reed" of Egypt were smashed.

After conquering the environs of the city, Sennacherib laid siege to Jerusalem itself. His own annals describe how he shut up Hezekiah "like a bird in a cage." Isaiah the prophet brought the one ray of hope. God would not allow Sennacherib so much as to shoot an arrow into the city. The city would be defended by the God of Israel.

Although Hezekiah paid an enormous indemnity to preserve Jerusalem—thirty talents of gold and 300 talents of silver—he retained his independence. The Assyrian army was smitten by the "angel of the Lord," so that Sennacherib had to flee home to Nineveh. Rebellion in Babylon and Elam demanded his attention so that it was some time before Sennacherib could plan a new invasion of the West. When he by-passed his elder sons to proclaim Esarhaddon, a son of his favorite wife, king, two of his sons killed him in the temple of Nisrok in Nineveh.

Some scholars, including John Bright (*A History of Israel,* pp. 269-271) suggest that Sennacherib made a second attack on Judah shortly before Hezekiah's death. If such an attack took place it was as futile as the first.

Hezekiah is regarded as one of the godly kings of Judah. He lived in critical times and, although he made serious mistakes, the nation was saved from ruin during his kingship. Had Sennacherib succeeded, Judah would have had a history parallel to that of Israel. This did not take place. Judah was spared until after the destruction of Nineveh and the Assyrian Empire.

CHAPTER 19

THE DARK DAYS OF MANASSEH AND AMON

CONTEMPORARY WITH ISAIAH, the prophet of Jerusalem, were Micah of Mareshah and Nahum of Elkosh. All three of these men declared the righteous judgments of God against Israel, Judah and Assyria. Nahum realistically described the impending downfall of Nineveh, the Assyrian capital from which destructive military campaigns annually sallied forth. Although a message of judgment, the announcement of the impending doom of Nineveh was one of hope for the oppressed people of western Asia.

With the passing from the scene of the generation which included Isaiah, Micah, Nahum and Hezekiah, a new period of calamity fell upon Judah. Her immediate problems were from within—a fresh turning from God to idols.

Manasseh. One of the most pious of Judah's kings was followed on the throne by one of the most impious. Hezekiah had never been friendly to Assyria, but at his death those who sought a closer relation with Assyria and her gods came into control. Manasseh was only twelve years of age when he became king. The court officials who counseled him were averse to the message of prophets such as Isaiah. The idol shrines which Hezekiah had destroyed were rebuilt. The Assyrian deities were added to those of Canaan in the popular cult. The Lord was still honored, but other gods were ranked with Him: "They prostrated before the Lord and swore by Milkom."

The Temple in Jerusalem was desecrated by the erection of altars "to the whole host of heaven." The worship of Ishtar, involving cultic prostitution by priestesses termed *qedeshoth,* was introduced into the Temple. Stalls were erected for the horses of Shamash, the sun god. Molech worship was revived, with a sanctuary built in his honor in the Valley of Hinnom, near Jerusalem. Manasseh sacrificed. his son to Molech there. Various types of superstition were revived—soothsaying, sorcery, necromancy. Assyrian customs were introduced and Assyrian dress became popular.

The spiritual impetus of the reform of Hezekiah was checked, but not completely obliterated. Prophets dared to proclaim God's imminent judgment on idolatrous Judah. Manasseh ordered a purge, filling Jerusalem with the blood of martyrs.

Esarhaddon, son and successor of Sennacherib, destroyed the city of Sidon and deported its population shortly after he came to the throne of Assyria. Tirhakah of Egypt was probably involved in the rebellion of Sidon. In a succession of campaigns, Esarhaddon marched against Egypt, finally occupying Memphis and the whole of Upper Egypt. Local governors were permitted to rule the land, responsible, of course, to Assyria.

In order to obviate the possibility of civil strife, Esarhaddon sought to provide a peaceful succession to the throne after his death. Assyria was alloted to Ashurbanipal and northern Babylon to Shamash-shum-ukin. Ashurbanipal retained control of the Empire, Shamash-shum-ukin being restricted to his Babylonian territory.

When Shamash-shum-ukin became dissatisfied with his secondary status he sought to incite Syria, Palestine and neighboring territories to throw off the Assyrian yoke. Manasseh sided with Shamash-shum-ukin against Ashurbanipal with disastrous results. Ashurbanipal took the city of Babylon by storm while Shamash-shum-ukin chose to perish in the flames of the burning palace rather than to fall into the hands of his irate brother.

For his part in the revolt "the captain of the host of the king of Assyria . . . took Manasseh with hooks and bound him with fetters and carried him to Babylon." The Senjirli Stele of Esarhaddon pictures one of his captives with a hook through his lips, tied by a rope to Esarhaddon's hands.

According to II Chronicles 33, Manasseh's experience in Babylon produced a spirit of repentance, after which he was permitted to return to Jerusalem. Ashurbanipal may have wished a grateful vassal in Judah because of its proximity to Egypt, a perennial trouble spot. With the permission of Ashurbanipal, Manasseh increased the fortifications of Jerusalem and manned the strongholds with garrisons. These moves were directed against Egypt, although they would later be of use in withstanding the attack of other foes.

On his return to Jerusalem, Manasseh sought to abolish the idolatry which he had fostered early in his reign. His reform efforts do not appear to have been very successful, however. The Book of Kings makes no mention of them and his son Amon seems to have been entirely unmoved.

Amon. The two years of Amon's reign were a repetition of the early policies of Manasseh. The altars to the false gods stood in the Temple courts and Baalism was rampant. In a palace conspiracy, the reason for which is not known, Amon was assassinated, leaving the throne to the eight-year-old Josiah.

CHAPTER 20

THE RULE OF JOSIAH

THE LIFETIME of the prophet Jeremiah spanned the years from Josiah to the Babylonian Exile. He had much the same function in his generation that Isaiah had a century earlier. Isaiah, however, could assure his generation that the Assyrian would not enter Jerusalem. Jeremiah spoke of imminent destruction at the hand of the Babylonians.

Josiah's Times. When Josiah came to the throne of Judah, Ashurbanipal was busy fighting in the eastern part of his empire. Following his victory over Shamash-shum-ukin he had to defend himself against the Elamites. Although victorious in the east, his strength was spent and subject peoples became more and more restive. Psammeticus I declared Egypt independent and founded the Twenty-sixth Dynasty. Ashurbanipal was powerless to intervene because of new problems in the north.

At the beginning of the seventh century a people known as the Scythians first appeared in the Near East from the region north of the Black Sea. Like the Huns and the Mongols who, centuries later, overran the west, the Scythians traveled in hordes, leaving desolation in their wake. Assyria had early made a treaty with them, but when they overran the Philistine country and approached the borders of Egypt, Assyria was powerless to intervene.

Another threat to the Assyrian power came from the Medes, a people who migrated from what is now southern Russia about 1000 B.C. and settled on the Iranian plateau. Another Aryan people, the Persians, settled farther south.

Assyrians fought with the Medes from the time of Shalmaneser III, but they would never remain permanently subjugated. The Medes had forced Esarhaddon to abandon his campaign in Egypt, and continued as a thorn in the side of Assyria.

In 625 B.C. a Chaldean, Nabopolassar, led a successful revolt against Assyria and founded the Neo-Babylonian Empire. The time of Assyria's greatness was clearly in the past, and it would be a short time before her very existence would be ended.

Josiah's Reforms. Early in the reign of Josiah he showed a disposition to turn from the idolatry of Manasseh and Amon and to honor the God of Israel. Both a result and a secondary cause of the reforms of Josiah was the discovery of the "Book of the Law of the Lord" in the Jerusalem Temple. Work of renovation and repair was going on when this book was found by Hilkiah, the priest. It was customary in ancient times to place contemporary articles in cornerstones. It is likely that Hilkiah came upon such a "foundation deposit," when investigating the need for Temple repair.

The book, which students suggest was Deuteronomy or other parts of the Mosaic Law, was taken to Shaphan, the scribe who brought it to Josiah and read it before the king.

When Josiah heard the threats of the law he sent to Huldah, the prophetess, in the hope of clarifying the matter. Huldah gave a message of encouragement and of judgment. Because Josiah had sought to live before his people in a godly manner, he would be spared from judgment. After Josiah's death, however, the threats contained in the Law would be fulfilled. The idolatry of Judah would be punished in a later generation.

Josiah's reaction was in harmony with his godly character. He called the people together, ordered the Book of the Law read in their hearing, and bound himself and the people to its observance by a solemn covenant. The Temple was cleansed, idolatry abolished, high places desecrated and the priests who functioned there ordered back to Jerusalem. A solemn observance of the Passover was held in Jerusalem at this time.

Josiah's reform had political overtones in that the abolition of the worship of foreign deities was an insult to the Assyrians, whose gods had been honored during the time of Manasseh and Amon. Josiah, however, had no need to fear retaliation. Assyria was busy elsewhere, and Josiah was pursuing a course of action which he was sure God would bless.

Battle of Megiddo. Following the death of Ashurbanipal the Assyrian Empire quickly approached its end. In 612 B.C. the city of Nineveh fell after being attacked by a coalition of Babylonians, Medes and Scythians. The remnants of the Assyrian army fled west to Haran and made it a temporary capital. Pharaoh-necho of Egypt, no lover of the Assyrians, came to their aid because of his greater fear of the growing Neo-Babylonian Empire.

On his way to join the Assyrians, Necho passed through Palestine. Josiah refused to permit peaceful passage for Necho, resulting in battle at the ancient fortress of Megiddo. There Josiah was mortally wounded. Although he had reigned for thirty-one years, he was under forty at the time of his death.

Carchemish.   At Carchemish on the Euphrates, Necho clashed with Nebuchadnezzar who was leading the armies of his father Nabopolassar, the Neo-Babylonian king. Carchemish was one of the world's decisive battles. In defeating an alliance of Egyptians and Assyrians, Nebuchadnezzar ended the power of two once strong peoples. Assyria passed away forever. Egypt aspired to leadership but never again became a first-rate power. The Babylonians were able to consolidate their gains and, after the death of Nabopolassar, Nebuchadnezzar became the ablest Mesopotamian ruler since Hammurabi, the lawgiver of the Old Babylonian Empire.

CHAPTER 21

THE LAST DAYS OF JUDAH

THE SONS AND SUCCESSORS of Josiah did not share the great reformer's zeal for the Lord. They lacked both religious zeal and political acumen, thereby hastening Judah to the doom which Huldah had prophesied.

Egyptian Control of Judah: Jehoahaz. The party in Judah which desired political independence succeeded in securing the throne for Jehoahaz, Josiah's second son. Necho, however, sought to retain control over Palestine for Egypt. He invited Jehoahaz to his headquarters at Riblah, deposed him and ordered his deportation to Egypt where he died after having been king for only three months.

Jehoiakim. Eliakim, or Jehoiakim, as he was subsequently named, had been by-passed as king in favor of his younger brother because of the anti-Egyptian element among the Judeans. Jehoiakim was known to be pro-Egyptian, and it was for this reason that Pharaoh-necho deposed Jehoahaz in his favor.

118

Determining to keep in the good graces of Necho, Jehoiakim levied heavy taxes on the people and turned them over to the Pharaoh.

The eleven years of Jehoiakim's reign were despotic. He built imposing buildings but impoverished the land through taxation, compulsory labor and plunder. The infamous high places began to be used and foreign deities again came into vogue. Jeremiah was threatened with death because he prophesied the impending judgments of the Lord. False prophets assured the king that God would never allow the heathen to desecrate His Temple, but Jeremiah insisted that calamity was impending.

After three years in Syria, Necho returned to Egypt and Nebuchadnezzar appeared to claim the lands which once were subject to Assyria. The kings of Syria readily acknowledged Nebuchadnezzar's sovereignty. Jehoiakim, however, played the part of an opportunist. At first professing loyalty to Nebuchadnezzar, he shifted to Necho when he felt it expedient to do so. Nebuchadnezzar, however, was not to be crossed. Jerusalem was besieged, and the first contingent of captives, including Daniel and his companions, were taken to Babylon. In the course of the events that followed, Jehoiakim seems to have been assassinated. He went unmourned and received the "burial of an ass" (Jer. 22:18, 19).

Jehoiachin. The young son of Jehoiakim, Jehoiachin succeeded his father to the throne which he occupied for ninety days. He was then deported to Babylon along with numerous leading citizens and artisans of Judah, including the prophet Ezekiel.

Jehoiachin was well treated in Babylon. Clay tablets record the quantity of oil delivered monthly to "Ja'ukinu, king of the land of Jaudi." After the death of Nebuchadnezzar, Evil-Merodach, the new Babylonian monarch, gave preferential treatment to Jehoiachin. He had a position "above the throne of the kings that were with him in Babylon" and was given special food and clothing allotments (II Kings 25:27 ff.).

Zedekiah. After taking Jehoiachin to Babylon, Nebuchadnezzar placed Mattaniah, renamed Zedekiah a son of Josiah and uncle of Jehoiachin on the throne of Judah. Zedekiah was a weak king, dominated by court officials whom he followed, frequently against his better judgment. He had good counsel from Jeremiah, whom he respected and feared even though he refused to follow the prophet's bidding.

Idolatry continued to be rampant during Zedekiah's reign. Canaanite, Babylonian, and Egyptian gods vied with the Lord for the loyalty of the people. Ezekiel from Babylon decried the moral depravity of Judah and insisted that the Glory of the Lord (i.e., the "glory cloud") would leave the Temple.

The pro-Egyptian party became more powerful, urging Zedekiah to seek help from Egypt and throw off the yoke of Nebuchadnezzar. In spite of Jeremiah's warning, Zedekiah applied to Pharaoh-hophra (Apries) for aid and the final revolt began.

Nebuchadnezzar's armies moved against Jerusalem. The patience of Nebuchadnezzar was exhausted. This time Jerusalem would not escape with the loss of gold and captives. Nothing less than complete destruction would suffice.

The appearance of Hophra's army brought a brief respite, and it appeared that Jeremiah might be wrong after all. Nebuchadnezzar made quick work of the Egyptians, however, and released his fury on Jerusalem once more. Pestilence, famine and cannibalism added to the horror of the siege. In 587 B.C. it was all over. Jerusalem fell to the might of Nebuchadnezzar.

Zedekiah tried to escape, but he was seized at Jericho and taken to Riblah to stand trial before Nebuchadnezzar. His sons were slain before his eyes, then he was blinded, fettered and taken to Babylon where he remained a prisoner until his death.

The destruction of Jerusalem was complete. The Temple furniture was sent to Babylon, after which the Temple itself was set on fire. The city was burned and the walls razed to eliminate the possibility of further revolt. The leading priests and citizens who had been active politically against Nebuchadnezzar were taken to Riblah and put to death. Then the masses were deported to Babylon.

The Aftermath. Nebuchadnezzar appointed Gedaliah, a prince who had been sympathetic with Jeremiah, as governor of the "poor of the land" who had not been taken into exile. Gedaliah ruled from Mizpah where he was supported by a small Babylonian garrison. Jeremiah himself chose to remain in Judah rather than accompany his people to Babylon as a free man.

Further trouble came, however, when a Judean official named Ishmael, related to the royal house, attempted to stage a further revolt. With the co-operation of Baalis, king of the Ammonites, Ishmael and his followers attacked and killed Gedaliah, his associates and the Babylonian garrison. Gedaliah had been warned of the plot but he refused to believe that Ishmael could be guilty of such an atrocity.

Ishmael expected to take the remaining inhabitants of Mizpah to Ammon, but he was overtaken by police units and forced to flee. The Jewish leaders, instead, migrated to Egypt, contrary to Jeremiah's advice. The prophet was taken with them and is thought to have died in Egypt. Jeremiah has been termed "the weeping prophet." Indeed, he was a man of strength, but no prophet has ever been more severely rejected by his own generation. It took the horrors of the destruction of Jerusalem and the captivity which followed to prove to the people that his message was true.

Habakkuk likewise prophesied during the last years of Jerusalem. We know nothing about his history, but his prophecy breathes the faith of one who looks beyond the present tragedy to the ultimate fulfillment of God's purposes. He sees the Chaldeans (or Babylonians) as the rod of God's wrath, but he also sees the day when judgment will fall on them for their sins.

Obadiah was particularly concerned because the Edomites, related to Israel through Esau, refused to afford a refuge for the Judeans as they fled southward to escape the wrath of Nebuchadnezzar. Edom rejoiced in the calamities of Judah, but God's judgment would soon fall on Edom.

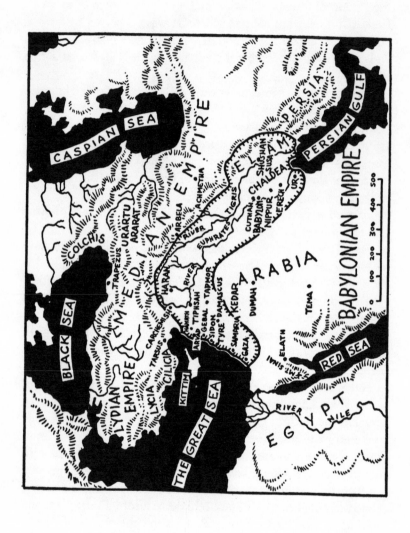

CHAPTER 22

THE JEWS IN BABYLON

THE END OF THE KINGDOM of Judah came in slow stages. Deportations took place during the reigns of Jehoiakim and Jehoiachin before the destruction of Jerusalem and the final deportation under Zedekiah. Remnants escaped to Egypt after Gedaliah, the governor appointed by the Babylonians, was murdered at Mizpah. Most of the inhabitants of Judah, however, were deported to Babylon and had to adjust to a new manner of life there.

In the experience of the Exile, ancient Israel lost its political sovereignty but gained its religious soul. The attractions of Baal and the Asherim which had proved fatal to pre-exilic Israel were left behind. Captivity was a humiliating experience, but it was the means of preparation for Israel's greatest period of blessing to mankind.

The Preservation of the Jew. With the period of the Exile the term "Jew" becomes significant. Strictly speaking, it refers to individuals of the tribe of Judah or inhabitants of the land occupied by that tribe, Judea. It came to be used of all

123

who traced their lineage, physical and spiritual, back to Abraham and owned the sacred Scriptures as their spiritual guide. "Israel" is the common designation of the pre-exilic descendants of Abraham, and "Jew" is used of those who returned from Babylon to rebuild on the old foundations.

The policy of the Assyrian conquerors of Samaria was such that the history of the Northern Kingdom, Israel, came to an abrupt end. The policy of transportation caused captive peoples to be scattered in various communities. Homes that were forsaken were occupied by those brought in from other areas. The possibility of a movement for return was thus eliminated.

The Babylonians, however, did not take the drastic measures used by their former masters. Judeans were taken to Babylon and they doubtless suffered great privation there. Yet they were permitted to dwell together in communities of their own. Ezekiel prophesied to a group of his countymen who lived in a place called Tell Abib by the River Chebar. Jeremiah urged his compatriots in Babylon to seek the peace of the city wherein they dwelt and to live as good citizens of the land. During Persian times we know of Jews who prospered in the land of their exile. It was providential that the Southern Kingdom was spared defeat by the Assyrians, for Babylonian policy permitted them to retain their national identity.

Employment in Babylon. We have only hints of the employment of the Jews in the land of their exile. Agriculture, the common means of livelihood in Palestine, was doubtless a major occupation. Jeremiah had urged the exiles to "plant gardens, and eat the fruit of them" (Jer. 29:28). Others however, found different means of livelihood. Daniel and his companions were trained to "stand before the king," i.e., to serve him in a governmental capacity. Daniel served as a kind of prime minister, while Shadrach, Meshach and Abednego had lesser, yet important functions in the state. Nehemiah was a cupbearer to the Persian king, another position involving responsibility. Among those who returned to Jerusalem at a later date were goldsmiths and apothecaries (Neh. 3:8). The clay tablets describing the activities of the Murashu family of Nippur give us a hint that Jews entered business during the Exile.

Religious Life. During the days before the Exile the worship of the Lord was regarded by many, both in and out of Israel, as a local cult. The new settlers in Samaria, after the capture of the city by Sargon, enlisted the aid of the priests of the Lord because they were told that the Lord was the God of the land of Israel. They worshiped Him along with the other gods which they brought with them. Ben-hadad had excused his defeat in the mountains of Samaria during the days of Ahab on the grounds that the gods of Israel were gods of the mountains. Naaman actually brought some soil from Israel back to Damascus with him that he might do homage to the God of Israel.

The Babylonian Exile forever removed the concept that the God of Israel could be localized. Judah was away from its land and its Temple. Yet its spiritual leaders saw the very Exile as a part of the plan of God to preserve and purify His people. The heathen might jeer at the weakness of Israel's God and His inability to save His people from the hand of Nebuchadnezzar. The godly Jew was convinced that God had delivered him into the hands of Nebuchadnezzar for high and holy purposes. The Temple might be in ruins, but the God of Israel was alive.

Although it cannot be said that the Jew was never guilty of idolatry again, nevertheless the Exile taught Israel the folly of idolatry. Just as the political reason for the Exile was the refusal of the last kings of Judah to pay tribute to Nebuchadnezzar, so the theological reason was the prevalence of idolatry among the pre-exilic Israelites. These concepts perfectly harmonized in the mind of the pious Jew during the Exile.

Babylonian idolatry was evident on every side to the captive Jew. He looked upon it with disgust. The very captivity tended to make him conscious of his national and spiritual heritage. Like Daniel, many Jews determined not to "defile themselves" with the religious rites of Babylon.

In the absence of Temple and sacrifice, particular emphasis

was placed upon Scripture during the Exile. Related to this love for the Torah (the Law), the institution of the synagogue and the office of the scribe arose.

The synagogue was non-existent in pre-exilic Judaism. The emphasis among the prophets and religious leaders was upon the unity of the God of Israel. A multiplicity of places of worship was related to a multiplicity of objects of worship, hence the abhorrence of the "high places" and the insistence on the one Jerusalem Sanctuary.

The situation of the Exile, however, produced the synagogue as a place for prayer and the study of Torah. It did not negate the concept of one Sanctuary. No sacrifices were offered in the synagogue, and when opportunity presented itself pious Jews returned to Jerusalem to build a Temple. The synagogue, however, proved a useful means of bringing together Jews for religious purposes not associated with animal sacrifice. Later Judaism decreed that a synagogue should be formed wherever there are ten Jewish families. The institution was kept by the Jews who returned to Palestine, and it continues as the focal point of Jewish corporate worship.

The scribes are mentioned as a profession from the time of Ezra through the New Testament period. Scribal activity seems to have begun during the Exile when attention was given to the study of Torah. In the first instance, copyists, the Scribes, became the "doctors" or teachers of the Law. Great emphasis was placed on the minutia of the Law, including sabbath observance, as a mark of the Jew in contrast to his pagan neighbors.

Language. The language spoken by pre-exilic Israel is known to us as Hebrew. It is a Semitic language closely related to the language spoken by the Canaanites of Ugarit, the Phoenicians, Moabites and other neighbors of Israel. The common language of the Jew in the period following the Exile was Aramaic, a sister Semitic tongue which has a history going back to patriarchal times. Laban was an Aramaean and the portion of the family which settled in the Haran area doubtless spoke the Aramaic tongue. It was used by the Aramaeans in their inscriptions. A form of Aramaic became the lingua franca of the Persian Empire. "Palestinian Aramaic" was the language of Christ and His disciples. Portions of Ezra, Nehemiah and Daniel are in Aramaic, as is the Jewish Talmud. The Targums were Aramaic translations or paraphrases of the Hebrew Scriptures.

Family Records. An experience such as the Babylonian Exile marked the end of national consciousness of many peo-ples of antiquity. The Jews, through love of their Law, pre-served themselves in the midst of an alien culture. Genealogies were carefully kept so that the Jews who returned from Babylon could, for the most part, tell both tribal and family relation-ships.

CHAPTER 23

BABYLON AND PERSIA

THE CITY OF JERUSALEM was destroyed in 587 B.C. by the Babylonians. About fifty years later the first group of colonists returned to Jerusalem with the co-operation of Cyrus, the Persian king. The power of the kingdom ruled by Nebuchadnezzar was great, but its duration short.

Nebuchadnezzar. Nebuchadnezzar was without doubt the most prominent figure of western Asia during the period of his rule. The kingdom which gained its independence under Nabopolassar, his father, became the unrivaled power of the Middle East under Nebuchadnezzar.

Best known from the Bible as a conqueror, much of Nebuchadnezzar's fame rested on his organization and building activities. The hanging gardens of Babylon were one of the wonders of the ancient world.

The Latter Kings of Babylon. It often happens that a powerful king is succeeded by weaklings. The successors of Nebuchadnezzar were unable to match the great Empire builder. Evil-Merodach (or Awil-Marduk, "man of Marduk"), the son and successor of Nebuchadnezzar, had a short and dissolute reign of two years. He is mentioned in II Kings 25 for the honor he bestowed on Jehoiachin of Judah, one of the captive kings residing in Babylon. Evil-Merodach was assassinated by his brother-in-law Nergalsharezer (or Neriglissar). This Nergalsharezer may be identified with the "Rab Mag" who was present with other high officers at the capture of Jerusalem (Jer. 39:3). He was among those who released Jeremiah from prison (Jer. 39:13).

After reigning four years Nergalsharezer was followed by his young son Labashi-Marduk, who was killed by a group of Babylonian nobles who conspired to seize the throne. One of these, Nabunaid (Nabonidus) took power as the final ruler of the Neo-Babylonian Empire.

Nabunaid was the last Semitic ruler to hold a position of world power. His interest in religion and archaeology, while commendable in itself, resulted in his disregard for the political demands of the Empire. He repaired the stage tower, or *ziggurat,* dedicated to the moon god, Sin, at Ur. One of his daughters, Bel-shalti-nannar, served as a priestess in the Ur temple. Another is said to have maintained a small museum of archaeological finds.

Nabunaid seriously neglected the defenses of Babylon. Babylonian armies became ineffective and the nation itself was without adequate defenses. When the capital was threatened, he is said to have imported gods into Babylon to protect the city.

Belshazzar. Cuneiform inscriptions make it clear that Belshazzar, described in Daniel 5 as the last king of Babylon, was the eldest son of Nabunaid. When Nabunaid found himself preoccupied with archaeological and theological pursuits he appointed his son Belshazzar as prince regent. He is described in Daniel 5 as a "son" of Nebuchadnezzar, in accord with Semitic usage which uses the term "son" of any male descendant and, in some instances, successors who are not in a blood relationship to the one presupposed as father. Belshazzar was in Babylon at the time the city fell to the Persians.

Cyrus the Persian. Cyrus succeeded to the throne of Anshan, an obscure Persian province, about 559 B.C. His rise to power was phenomenal. Within ten years he had united his own people and conquered the Medes. Thus the term Medo-Persian is sometimes used of the empire of Cyrus. Three years later the kingdom of Lydia, in Asia Minor, was a part of the Persian Empire, a prize which brought Cyrus into contact with the Greeks.

Having subdued lands to the east and west of Babylon, Cyrus turned upon the domain of Nabunaid and Belshazzar. As a matter of fact, Cyrus was able to take advantage of popular discontent at the policies of Nabunaid and pose as a liberator. No serious opposition was encountered by his army. Belshazzar, the prince regent who was in the city when Cyrus' general Gubaru took Babylon, was slain. The Book of Daniel names a "Darius the Mede" as the ruler of Babylon after it fell to the Medo-Persian Empire. The identity of this "Darius the Mede" has been a thorny historical problem. Some scholars dismiss the reference as a historical error in which Daniel has chronologically misplaced Darius the Great (Hystaspes). Conservatives tend to identify "Darius the Mede" with Gubaru (Gobryas) who is known to have appointed governors in Babylon after the fall of the city.

CHAPTER 24

THE RETURN FROM EXILE

THE DECREE OF CYRUS. The conquest of Babylon by the
armies of Cyrus brought important changes to the Jews
and to other captive peoples. Reversing the policy of the Neo-
Babylonian kings, Cyrus made it his policy to restore captive
peoples and return the gods which had been brought into Babylon to their proper shrines. Although the Jews had no image
to be returned to Jerusalem they did have vessels used in Temple worship which had been taken to Babylon by Nebuchadnezzar.

Cyrus issued a decree ordering that the Jerusalem Temple be
restored and that the sacred vessels be returned (Ezra 6:3-5).
The Jews were permitted to return for the task of rebuilding the
Temple with the assurance of assistance along the way (Ezra
1:2-4). Under the leadership of a Jewish prince who had been
appointed governor of Judah, Sheshbazzar, about 50,000 Jews
made the long trek from Babylon to Jerusalem. Aside from
the assertion that he "laid the foundation of the house of God
which is in Jerusalem" we read no more of Sheshbazzar. The
names of Zerubbabel as civil leader and Joshua (or Jeshua) the
priest subsequently appear as leaders of the Jews in Jerusalem.
In accord with the decree of Cyrus they built the Altar of Burnt
Offering and restored the daily morning and evening sacrifices

which had been suspended since the destruction of Jerusalem. Nothing more was accomplished in the work of rebuilding the Temple during the lifetime of Cyrus.

Opposition from the "Adversaries of Judah and Benjamin."

Although the Babylonians had not settled captive peoples in Jerusalem as the Assyrians had done in Samaria, there were numerous peoples who were settled in the neighborhood of Jerusalem who did not welcome the return of the Jews. These included the Samaritans who had been settled in territory once belonging to the kingdom of Israel, and Edomites, or Idumaeans as they were subsequently called, who had been pushed by the Nabataean Arabs from their former home south of the Dead Sea into the Judaean highlands, the Negev and southern Judah as far north as Hebron. North of the Edomites a people known as Calebites occupied territory up to Bethlehem.

These peoples had profited from the expulsion and deportation of Judah by Nebuchadnezzar. They could not be expected to hail the returning pilgrims with enthusiasm.

One effort was made by the Samaritans to co-operate with the Jews. Alleging that they had been worshipers of the God of Israel since they had been introduced to the land as a result of Esarhaddon's deportation, they offered to assist in the work of rebuilding the Temple. They seem to have shared the common concept that each land has its distinctive God, and that the Lord should be honored by those who lived in Israel, His land.

The Jews were not convinced of the purity of the faith of the Samaritans, however. Making reference to the decree of Cyrus, which had authorized the Jews to rebuild the Temple, they disclaimed any reason for accepting Samaritan help.

After this rebuff, the "people of the land" used every conceivable means to hinder the Jews from completing their task. They did not resort to open warfare, probably because of the power of the Persian Empire which had authorized assistance to the Jews. Ezra notes that the adversaries "troubled them in building," restoring to guerrilla warfare tactics and making insinuations before the Persian court that the rebuilding of Jerusalem was planned by Jews who had ulterior motives.

The adversaries were temporarily successful. For about eighteen years no progress was made. In the meantime Cyrus died, being succeeded first by his son Cambyses, who invaded Egypt and added it to the Persian Empire, and then by Darius the Great. Joyful enthusiasm on the part of those who first returned to Jerusalem gave way to disillusionment and frustration. The prophets Haggai and Zechariah were used of God in challenging the people to believe God and press on in obedience to His will.

CHAPTER 25

EZRA AND NEHEMIAH

W E HAVE LITTLE HISTORICAL INFORMATION for the years between the completion of the Temple and the coming of Ezra and his company to Jerusalem. Jews were expected to supply troops for the campaigns of Xerxes and Artaxerxes against Egypt. They paid heavy tribute to the Persian Empire and their own economic position was very low. Small farmers who were unable to repay their loans would lose their land and, in some instances, their liberty and that of their families. The wealthy increased their possessions, and the poor were increasing in poverty.

Contacts with the neighboring peoples, Samaritans, Moabites and Phoenicians, grew more cordial. Not only business dealings, but mixed marriages became prevalent, due largely to the fact that more men than women had returned from Babylon. Children of these mixed marriages did not speak Hebrew, an indication of the low regard for Jewish life on the part of their non-Jewish mothers.

The Jewish Law was generally neglected. Business was transacted on the sabbath day, and the prophets speak of murder, adultery, perjury, lying and injustice in the courts. False prophets were more interested in material gain than in declaring the truth of God. It is significant that both Ezra and Nehemiah came from the dispersion, the term used of the non-Palestinian Jews from the time of the Exile to the present.

Ezra. Ezra, a descendant of the high priest Seraiah, whom Nebuchadnezzar had put to death at the capture of Jerusalem, is termed a "scribe," probably an official court title designating Ezra's responsibility for Jewish affairs at the Persian court. The name subsequently was applied to Jewish copyists and students of the Law, a subject in which Ezra is said to have had much skill.

Concerned about the spiritual condition of Palestinian Jewry, Ezra led a company of 1500 men with their families to the Holy City. He brought with him gold and silver to be used for the expenses of the priests and the Temple.

On arrival in Jerusalem, Ezra was grieved at the laxity of the people toward the Law. He assembled them together and read "the Book of the Law of Moses," commenting on it and explaining it in the language of the people (Aramaic). Those who heard the Law were moved, realizing how far they had strayed from the standards which God had set before His people at Sinai. The Feast of Tabernacles was observed, with a reading of the Law each day of the feast.

A problem which particularly vexed Ezra was that of mixed marriages. Solomon had been led into idolatry by his foreign wives, and the marriage of Ahab to Jezebel had precipitated a crisis in the religious life of the Northern Kingdom. Athaliah had brought Baalism to Judah. Now Ezra saw a similar tragedy facing post-exilic Judaism.

A decree was issued ordering the people to appear in Jerusalem under penalty of excommunication and confiscation of property. On the day set, Ezra demanded the dissolution of all mixed marriages. A commission would be appointed to deal with disputed cases.

Although numerous mixed marriages were dissolved and the reform of Ezra seemed successful, serious opposition came from some in the higher circles of the priesthood. Samaritans and other peoples whose daughters were dismissed from Jewish homes were understandably resentful. To defend Jerusalem from possible attack, Ezra began to rebuild the city's walls. The Samaritans informed Artaxerxes of this act which could be considered as treason against Persia. Samaritans marched upon Jerusalem and tore down the section of the wall which had been rebuilt. It is thought that Ezra returned to Persia and reported the course of events to the king.

Nehemiah. Babylonian Jews were disheartened at the news of the difficulties which faced their compatriots in Jerusalem. Nehemiah, the cupbearer in the court of Artaxerxes, received from the king royal approval for his plan of rebuilding the walls. Perhaps the king was swayed by considerations of his own security. A strong citadel close to the Egyptian border in the hands of a friendly people would be an asset to Persia.

Empowered to proceed with the building of the walls, Nehemiah was given a leave of absence from his royal duties to make a trip to Jerusalem. After surveying the broken-down walls of the city, Nehemiah presented his plans for reconstruction to the elders of Jerusalem and gained their approval. The work was divided into units and the people assigned their task in the total project.

Difficulties again came from the perennial adversaries. Sanballat, governor of Samaria, Geshem the Arabian and the "Horonites" (probably from Beth-horon in Samaria) resorted first to ridicule and then to force in their attempt to stop the work. Nehemiah posted guards and admonished the builders to be constantly ready to fight.

When they could not entice Nehemiah to a parley in order to convince him that he should abandon his plan, the Samaritans and their allies spread the rumor that Nehemiah was planning an insurrection and was seeking to make himself king. A false prophet was employed to urge Nehemiah to pass the night in the Temple to safeguard himself from attack.

All of these efforts of Nehemiah's adversaries proved futile. Because "the people had a mind to work," the walls were finished and solemnly dedicated to God. In order to protect the city Nehemiah arranged for the transfer of Jews from the surrounding countryside into Jerusalem.

Nehemiah, the layman, and Ezra, the priest and scribe, were

both concerned for the spiritual and the material well-being of
Judah. After fortifying Jerusalem, Nehemiah gave his attention to spiritual problems. Economic oppression, sabbath dese-
cration, and mixed marriages vexed him as they vexed Ezra.
Nehemiah assembled the people who declared themselves ready
to obey the Law of God. When Jehoiada, the son of the high
priest, objected to giving up his foreign wife (a daughter of
Sanballat), Nehemiah drove him out of the city.

It is known that Nehemiah made at least two visits to Jerusalem (Neh. 13:6). The chronology of the period of Ezra and
Nehemiah is a subject of considerable scholarly discussion.
While not without problems, the priority of Ezra to Nehemiah
seems best to accord with the Biblical evidence.

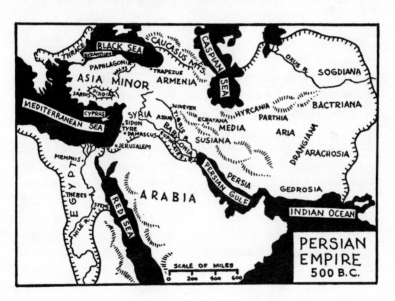

CHAPTER 26

A CHAPTER FROM PERSIAN JEWRY

ONE SMALL BOOK of the Old Testament gives us a glimpse of the Jews who did not return to Palestine, their trials and their victories under a Persian king. The Book of Esther does not mention the name of God, but it does bear witness to God's concern for His people, wherever they might be.

Ahasuerus. The Ahasuerus of the Book of Esther is identified by many as the Persian king Xerxes I, the successor of Darius the Great. Xerxes is known in history largely because of his unsuccessful invasion of Greece. Under the celebrated Themistocles, the Greeks defeated the Persian fleet at Salamis, one of the decisive battles of history. Xerxes returned to Persia, leaving his general, Mardonius, behind to direct the Persian forces. Mardonius saw the Persians defeated on land at Plataea in Boeotia and at sea at Mycale in Asia Minor on one and the same day.

Xerxes did not distinguish himself on the field of battle after the Greek debacle. He had the reputation of acting like a spoiled child, a characteristic which fits in well with his description in the Book of Esther. There, when Vashti refused to make a lewd display of herself, he deposed her and sought a suitable queen from among the fairest women of his realm.

Susa or Shushan. The royal palace in the Book of Esther is at Shushan, or Susa, a city in the mountainous part of the province of Elam, or Susiana. Susa was the royal winter palace of the Persian kings, as Ecbatana was the summer palace.

Excavations at Susa have brought to light bricks and pavements begun by Darius I and enlarged by his successors. The palace had three courts surrounded by rooms decorated with panels of glazed bricks showing spearmen and symbolic winged bulls and griffins.

Esther and Mordecai. After the removal of the virtuous Vashti from her position as queen, the beautiful Jewish maiden, Esther, became queen to Ahasuerus. Mordecai, cousin and foster father to Esther, learned of a plot to kill the king and informed Esther, thus saving the life of Ahasuerus. He angered Haman, the king's favorite, however, by refusing to reverence him.

Haman influenced Ahasuerus to order the destruction of all the Jews in the Empire that he might kill Mordecai. In the meantime, during a sleepless night Ahasuerus ordered the royal chronicles to be read to him and was reminded of the fact that he had not honored Mordecai for his act of saving the king's life. Haman, who thought the king desired to honor him rather than his hated enemy, Mordecai, suggested that the king might honor the one of his choice by arraying him in royal apparel and leading him through the streets. Haman, then, was ordered to honor Mordecai in this way.

At a royal banquet Esther named Haman as the enemy of her people, and Ahasuerus ordered him hanged on the gallows which he had earlier prepared for Mordecai. Esther revealed her relationship to Mordecai who received a position second only to the king. Although the decree to exterminate the Jews could not be revoked, they were permitted to defend themselves. The result was the deliverance of the Jews and the destruction of large numbers of their enemies. The deliverance of the Jews through the courage of Esther is commemorated annually at the Jewish Feast of Purim.

CHAPTER 27

ALEXANDER AND HELLENISM

WHILE THE LAST positive historical references in the Old Testament are to the period during which the Persian Empire ruled the Middle East, a brief discussion of subsequent events may prove helpful to the student of Bible history. The latter Persian kings did not distinguish themselves. The effort to conquer Greece was never successful and, ultimately, the tide of empire moved in the opposite direction when Alexander, the son and heir of Philip of Macedon, crossed the Hellespont and invaded Asia Minor.

Alexander secured permanent hold of Macedonia and then entered Greece where he became master of the country in short order. Alexander loved Greece, its culture and people. Aristotle had been his tutor, so he had early learned of the Trojan War and had been impressed with the thought of bringing Greek culture to the less enlightened peoples. Alexander was a conqueror, but he was also a kind of missionary—a missionary of Hellenism, the Greek way of doing things.

Alexander's Conquests. After securing control of Greece, Alexander crossed into Asia where he encountered and defeated Persian forces at the River Granicus, in western Asia Minor, and at Issus in Cilicia. Passing through Syria and Palestine he pressed on toward Egypt. Tyre withstood him for several months, but he finally brought about its submission by constructing a mole to connect the ruins of the ancient city on the mainland with the modern city on the adjacent island.

Alexander probably passed down the Philistine plain without stopping at Jerusalem, although tradition suggests that he was met by a procession of friendly priests there who so impressed him that he spared the city. Egypt was rapidly subdued. Alexander was proclaimed a god and thus a legitimate successor to the ancient Pharaohs. The most famous of many Alexandrias which he built was in Egypt. It subsequently became the cultural center of the Hellenistic world and boasted a large Jewish population.

From Egypt, Alexander backtracked into Asia, moving northward through Palestine and Syria, and then down the Tigris-Euphrates Valley. In the Battle of Arbela, not far from ancient Nineveh, Alexander struck the deathblow to the Persian Empire. From Cyrus, its first king, to Darius III, its last, was a period of about two centuries.

After conquering Persia, Alexander determined to move farther east where he penetrated into the Punjab region of India. He doubtless would have gone on, had not his Macedonian soldiers refused. They had been away from home for eleven years and determined to head westward. Alexander never reached home, however. At the age of thirty-two he died in the city of Babylon. A veteran of many battles, he died of a fever brought on or aggravated by drinking to excess at a banquet.

Alexander's Successors. Alexander left no heir except the infant son of a Bactrian princess whom he had married. His generals, however, determined to reap the fruit of their labors. After a series of internal struggles, Alexander's empire was divided among four generals: Ptolemy, Lysimachus, Cassander and Seleucus. Egypt fell to Ptolemy and, during the early years following the division of the empire, Palestine was ruled by the Ptolemies.

The Ptolemies. The Jews fared well both in Palestine and in Egypt under the Ptolemies. Under Ptolemy Philadelphus the Egyptian Jews began the translation of their Scriptures into the Greek language, the version which became known as the Septuagint. Philadelphus is also known for the building of the lighthouse of Pharos, one of the wonders of the ancient world, and the great library of Alexandria, a collection of books from all nations. The seaport of Acco, or Ptolemais (modern Acre), was built on the coast of Palestine north of Mount Carmel.

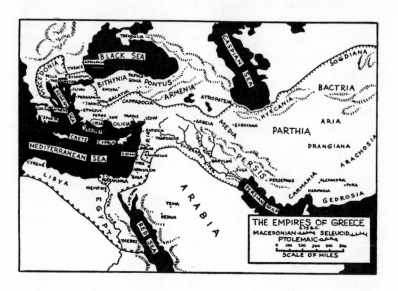

The Seleucids. The rulers of Syria are named for Seleucus, one of Alexander's generals who ultimately acquired nearly all of Asia for his dominion. New cities were built as his eastern and western capitals—Seleucia on the Euphrates about forty miles from Babylon, and Antioch on the Orontes River in Syria (named after his father, Antiochus).

Palestine was a buffer state between the Ptolemies and the Seleucids of the Hellenistic age as it had been between the Egyptians and the Babylonians or Assyrians of earlier history. During the reign of the Seleucid ruler Antiochus the Great,

Syria and Palestine were taken from Egypt and added to the Syrian kingdom after a series of battles.

The Seleucid rule of Palestine is one of the blackest of history. The Hellenistic party of Jews was eager to discard all in their religious heritage which hindered the acceptance of the new Greek culture. The Pious, or Hasidim as they are called, rejected Hellenism as a challenge to the faith of Judaism. Before the intervention of the Syrians the Jews experienced their own inner struggle which, in one form or another, continued until the destruction of Jerusalem in A.D. 70.

Under Antiochus, surnamed Epiphanes, the Syrians attempted to proscribe Judaism in its orthodox form, throwing their weight behind the Hellenistic party among the Jews. This was motivated by the military and economic necessities of the occasion, but Antiochus showed an utter disregard for the feelings of the orthodox. He entered the Holy of Holies in the Jerusalem Temple and desecrated it. He sacrificed a sow on the Altar of Burnt Offering. Sabbath observance and circumcision were outlawed. It was clearly the purpose of Antiochus to unify his empire by eliminating all religious differences. This would mean the destruction of Judaism.

CHAPTER 28

REVOLT OF THE MACCABEES

THE EXTREMES to which Antiochus Epiphanes went in his attempt at destroying Judaism brought about a violent reaction. The party of the Pious (*Hasidim*) determined to resist to the death the measures designed to eradicate Judaism.

Mattathias. A godly priest at Modin, in the Philistine Plain west of Jerusalem, Mattathias challenged Antiochus. He not only refused to sacrifice before a pagan altar, he also killed a Jew who stepped up to do so, along with the emissary of Antiochus who was seeking to bring about conformity to the royal decree. With his five sons, aged Mattathias fled to the Judean mountains where he waged guerrilla warfare with the Syrians.

Judas the Maccabee. At the death of Mattathias the leadership of the revolt was entrusted to his son Judah, or Judas. Many of the faithful among the Jews had joined in the revolt. The Syrians attempted to subdue the rebels but were unable to do so. Three campaigns were fought, but the Jews were victorious in each one. Finally civil war at home forced the Syrians to conclude peace with the Jews. Judas the Maccabee caused the Temple to be purged and rededicated and the ancient ritual

144

to be reinstituted. Religious liberty had been obtained and many of the Jews were satisfied. Judas wanted to press on to full political freedom, but he was in the minority. Attacked by the Syrians again, Judas died in battle, a martyr to the cause of Jewish independence.

The Brothers of Judas. Jonathan, a brother of Judas, succeeded him as leader of the revolt. Owing to internal troubles in Syria, Jonathan was able to get his authority recognized and was declared commander of Judea. Another brother, Simon, succeeded Jonathan. The sovereignty over Judah was made hereditary in the house of Simon, who was succeeded by his son, John Hyrcanus.

The Later Hasmonaeans. Under John Hyrcanus the old differences between the Hellenists and the Pious again asserted themselves. First associated with the Pious, Hyrcanus later changed his loyalties and sided with the Hellenistic party. At this time the party names familiar in the New Testament appear. The Hellenists become the party of the Sadducees, and the Pious become the Pharisees. Many of the things which Mattathias and his sons fought for were lost by the later Hasmonaeans, the name given to the dynasty established by Simon.

Under Aristobulus, son of Hyrcanus, and his brother, Alexander Jannaeus, wars of conquest and bitter internal strife between the Pharisees and the Sadducees were commonplace. Aristobulus was the first of the Maccabees to call himself king. Since he was not of the Davidic line this was resented by the orthodox.

Salome Alexandra, the widow successively of Aristobulus and Jannaeus, ruled after the death of the latter. Sympathetic with the Pharisees, her reign was one which brought about numerous changes pleasing to the Pious in Israel. As Aristobulus and Jannaeus had shed Pharisee blood, however, Sadducean blood flowed during the reign of Alexandra. At her death civil war broke out between her sons, Aristobulus II and Hyrcanus II. Pompey, who was in the east when hostilities began between the two brothers, intervened (63 B.C.). Roman legions besieged Jerusalem, after which Pompey captured it and entered the Holy of Holies. The Jewish state became subject to Rome.

Chart of the Divided Kingdom

Kings of Judah	Events and Prophets	Date	Kings of Assyria or Babylonia	Kings of Israel
Rehoboam	Shishak's invasion	925		Jeroboam I
Abijam				
Asa			Adad-nirari II	
				Nadab
	Asa allies with Ben-hadad of Syria against Baasha.	900	Tukulti-ninurta II	Baasha
				Elah
			Ashurnasirpal II	Zimri
Jehoshaphat	Elijah prophesies	875		Omri
				Ahab
	Battle of Karkar		Shalmaneser III	Ahaziah
Jehoram	Elisha prophesies	850		Jehoram
				Jehu
Ahaziah (Athaliah)	Jehu pays tribute to Shalmaneser	825	Shamshi-adad V	
				Jehoahaz
Joash	Hazael oppresses Judah			Joash
Amaziah		800	Adad-nirari III	
				Jeroboam II
Uzziah			Shalmaneser IV	
	Hosea			
	Amos	775		
	Jonah		Ashur-dan III	
	Isaiah			
Jotham			Ashur-nirari I	Zachariah
		750		Shallum
	Micah		Tiglath-pileser III (Pul)	Menahem
				Pekahiah
Ahaz	Joel (?)			Pekah
	Obadiah (?)	725	Shalmaneser V	Hoshea
Hezekiah			Sargon II	(Fall of
			Sennacherib	Samaria,
				722 B.C.)

Kings of Judah	Events and Prophets	Date	Kings of Assyria or Babylonia	Kings of Israel
	Sennacherib invades Judah	700		
Manasseh			Esarhaddon	
	Assyria fights Egypt	675	Ashurbanipal	
	Manasseh carried to Babylon	650	Ashur-etil-ilanu Sin-shar-ishkun	
Amon			Nabopolassar establishes Neo-Babylonian Empire	
Josiah	Nahum Zephaniah Jeremiah Fall of Nineveh (612) Josiah killed at Megiddo (608)	625		
Jehoahaz	Carchemish (605)		Nebuchadnezzar	
Jehoiakim	Habakkuk			
Jehoiachin		600		
Zedekiah (Fall of Jerusalem, 587 B.C.)	Ezekiel Daniel			

KINGS OF BABYLON AND PERSIA

625 B.C. Nabopolassar, founder of the Neo-Babylonian
Empire
605 Nebuchadnezzar, son of Nabopolassar
562 Evil-Merodach, son of Nebuchadnezzar
560 Neriglissar, brother-in-law to Evil-Merodach
556 Nabunaid (Nabonidus), a usurper who overthrew
the dynasty of Nabopolassar. During his last years
his son Belshazzar served as Prince Regent.
538 Cyrus the Persian conquers Babylon
530 Cambyses, son of Cyrus
522 Darius Hystaspes or "Darius the Great"
486 Xerxes, son of Darius (Ahasuerus)
464 Artaxerxes, son of Xerxes
423 Darius II
404 Artaxerxes II
359 Artaxerxes III
338 Arses
335 Darius III
334-323 Alexander the Great conquers Asia

BIBLIOGRAPHY

Recommended Works in Old Testament History

Abel, F. M., *Histoire de la Palestine* (Paris: J. Gabalder, 1952).

Adams, James McKee, *Ancient Records and the Bible* (Nashville 3, Tenn.: Broadman Press, 1946).

————, *Biblical Backgrounds* (Nashville 3: Broadman Press, 1938).

Albright, W. F., *Archaeology and the Religion of Israel* (Baltimore 18: Johns Hopkins Press, 1942).

————, *The Archaeology of Palestine* (Harmondsworth, Middlesex, England: Penguin Books, 1954).

————, *From the Stone Age to Christianity* (Baltimore: Johns Hopkins Press, 1946).

Anderson, B. W., *Understanding the Old Testament* (New York 11: Prentice-Hall, Inc., 1957).

Baikie, J., *The Amarna Age* (London, W. 1: A. & C. Black, 1926).

Bailey, A. E., *Daily Life in Bible Times* (New York 17: Charles Scribner's Sons, 1943).

Bailey, A. E., and Kent, C. F., *History of the Hebrew Commonwealth* (New York 17: Charles Scribner's Sons, 1920).

Barton, G. A., *Archaeology and the Bible* (Philadelphia 3: American Sunday School Union, 1937).

Beek, M. A., *A Journey Through the Old Testament* (London, E.C. 4: Hodder & Stoughton, 1959).

Bertholet, A., *A History of Hebrew Civilization* (London, W.C. 1: George C. Harrap & Co. 1926).

Bevan, C. R., and Singer, C., editors, *The Legacy of Israel* (London, E.C. 4: Clarendon Press, 1928).

Blaikie, W. G., rev. by C. D. Matthews, *A Manual of Bible History* (New York 17: Thomas Nelson & Sons, 1940).

Breasted, J. H., *Ancient Records of Egypt* (Chicago 37: University of Chicago Press, 1906-07).

Bright, John, *A History of Israel* (Philadelphia 7: The Westminster Press, 1959).

————, *Early Israel in Recent History Writing* (Naperville, Ill.: Alec R. Allenson, Inc., 1956).

Bruce, F. F., *The Hittites and the Old Testament* (London, W.C. 1: Tyndale Press [Inter-varsity]) 1947.

Burrows, M., *What Mean These Stones?* (Yale Sta., New Haven: American Schools of Oriental Research, 1941).

Bury, J. B., Cook, S. A., and Adcock, F. E., editors, *Cambridge Ancient History* (London, N.W. 1: Cambridge University Press, 1928-1954).

Caiger, S. L., *Bible and Spade* (Oxford: Oxford University Press, 1954).

———, *The Old Testament and Modern Discovery* (Oxford, E.C. 4, Oxford University Press, 1933).

Ceram, C. W., *Gods, Graves, and Scholars* (New York 22: Alfred A. Knopf, 1954).

———, *The Secret of the Hittites* (New York 22: Alfred A. Knopf, 1956).

Chiera, E., *They Wrote on Clay* (Chicago 37: University of Chicago Press, 1938).

Childe, V. G., *What Happened in History* (Harmondsworth, Middlesex, England: Penguin Books, rev. ed., 1954).

Clay, A. T., *Amurru—The Home of the Northern Semites* (Philadelphia: Sunday School Times, 1909).

Cooke, G. A., *A Textbook of North Semitic Inscriptions* (Oxford: Clarendon Press, 1903).

———, *The Religion of Ancient Palestine in the Light of Archaeology* (London, E.C. 4: Oxford University Press, 1930).

Cowley, A. E., *Aramaic Papyri of the Fifth Century B.C.* (Oxford: Clarendon Press, 1923).

Daniel-Rops, H., *Sacred History* (New York 3: Longmans Green & Co., 1949).

DeBurgh, W. G., *The Legacy of the Ancient World* (New York 11: The Macmillan Co., 1924).

DeVaux, Roland, *Ancient Israel: Its Life and Institutions,* (New York: McGraw-Hill Book Company, 1961).

Dentan, R. C., *The Idea of History in the Ancient Near East* (New Haven 7, Conn.: Yale University Press, 1955).

Duncan, J. Garrow, *Digging Up Biblical History* (London, W.C. 2: Society for Promoting Christian Knowledge, 1931).

Dupont, Sommer, A., *Les Arameens* (Paris: A. Maissoneuve, 1954).

Edwards, I. E. S., *The Pyramids of Egypt* (Harmondsworth, Middlesex, England: Penguin Books, 1947).

Erman, A., *Life in Ancient Egypt* (London, W.C. 2: The Macmillan Co., 1894).

————, *The Literature of the Ancient Egyptians* (London, W.C. 2: A. Methuen & Co., 1927).

Finegan, J., *Light from the Ancient Past* (Princeton, N. J.: Princeton University Press, 2nd edition, 1959).

Finkelstein, L., ed., *The Jews: Their History, Culture, and Religion* (Philadelphia 2: Jewish Publication Society, 1949).

Frankfort, Henri, *The Birth of Civilization in the Near East* (London, W.C. 1: Williams & Norgate, 1951).

Free, J. P., *Archaeology and Bible History* (Wheaton, Van Kampen Press, 1950).

Garstang, J., *The Foundations of Bible History: Joshua, Judges* (London, W.C. 2: Constable & Co., 1931).

Ghirshman, R., *Iran* (Harmondsworth, Middlesex, England: Penguin Books, 1954).

Glueck, N., *The Other Side of the Jordan* (New Haven, Yale Sta.: American Schools of Oriental Research, 1940).

————, *The River Jordan* (Philadelphia 7: Westminster Press, 1946).

————, *Rivers in the Desert* (New York 3: Farrar, Straus, & Cudahy, 1959).

Goodspeed, G. S., *History of the Babylonians and Assyrians* (New York 17: Charles Scribner's Sons, 1917).

Gordon, C. H., *Adventures in the Near East* (Fair Lawn, N. J.: Essential Books Inc., 1957).

————, *Ugaritic Literature* (Rome: Pontifical Biblical Institute, 1949).

————, *The World of the Old Testament* (New York 22: Doubleday & Co., 1958).

Gottwald, Norman K., *A Light to the Nations* (New York 16: Harper & Brothers, 1959).

Grollenberg, L., *Atlas of the Bible* (New York 17: Thomas Nelson & Sons, 1956).

Gurney, O. R., *The Hittites* (Harmondsworth, Middlesex, England: Penguin Books, 1952).

Hall, H. R. H., *The Ancient History of the Near East* (London, W.C. 2: Methuen & Co., 1950).

Harding, G. Lankaster, *The Antiquities of Jordan* (London, E.C. 4: Lutterworth Press, 1957).

Harrison, R. K., *A History of Old Testament Times* (Grand Rapids 6: Zondervan Publishing House, 1957).

Heaton, E. W., *Everyday Life in Old Testament Times* (New York 17: Charles Scribner's Sons, 1956).

Heidel, A., *The Babylonian Genesis* (Chicago 37: University of Chicago Press, 1951).

———, *The Gilgamesh Epic and Old Testament Parallels* (Chicago 37: University of Chicago Press, 1949).

Heinisch, P., tr., Heidt, W., *History of the Old Testament* (Collegeville, Minn.: Liturgical Press, 1952).

Hitti, P. K., *History of Syria Including Lebanon and Palestine* (New York 11: The Macmillan Co., 1951).

Jack, J. W., *The Date of the Exodus* (Edinburgh 2: T. & T. Clark, 1925).

Kaufmann, Y., *The Biblical Account of the Conquest of Palestine* (Jerusalem: Hebrew University, 1953).

Keller, W., *The Bible as History* (New York 16: William Morrow & Co., 1956).

Kent, C. F., *A History of the Hebrew People: The Divided Kingdom* (New York 17: Charles Scribner's Sons, 1903).

———, *A History of the Hebrew People: The United Kingdom* (New York 17: Charles Scribner's Sons, 1903).

———, *A History of the Jewish People: Babylonian and Greek Periods* (New York 17: Charles Scribner's Sons, 1899).

Kenyon, F. G., *The Bible and Archaeology* (New York 16: Harper & Brothers, 1940).

Kenyon, K. M., *Beginning in Archaeology* (New York 36: Frederick A. Praeger, 1952).

———, *Digging Up Jericho* (New York 36: Frederick A. Praeger, 1957).

King, L. W., *History of Sumer and Akkad* (London, W.C. 2: Chatto & Windus, 1910).

Kraeling, E. G., *Aram and Israel* (New York 27: Columbia University Press, 1918).

———, *Rand-McNally Bible Atlas* (New York: Rand McNally & Co., [Chicago 80] 1956).

Kramer, S. N., *From the Tablets of Sumer* (Indian Hills, Colo.: Falcon's Wing Press, 1956).

Leslie, E. A., *Old Testament Religion in the Light of its Canaanite Background* (Nashville 2: Abingdon Cokesbury, 1936).

Lloyd, Seton, *Foundations in the Dust* (Harmondsworth, Middlesex, England: Penguin Books, 1955).

Lods, A., *Israel* (London, E.C. 4: Kegan, Paul, Trubner & Co., 1932).

Luckenbill, D. D., *Ancient Records of Assyria and Babylonia* (Chicago 37: University of Chicago Press, 1926).

Macalister, R. A. S., *A History of Civilization in Palestine* (Cambridge, N.W. 1, England: Cambridge University Press, 1912).

McCown, C. C., *The Ladder of Progress in Palestine* (New York 16: Harper & Brothers, 1943).

———, *Man, Morals, and History* (New York 16: Harper & Brothers, 1958).

Meek, T. J., *Hebrew Origins* (New York 16: Harper & Brothers, 1950).

Mendelsohn, I., ed., *Religions of the Ancient Near East* (New York 23: Liberal Arts Press, 1955).

Mercer, S. A. B., *Extra-Biblical Sources for Hebrew and Jewish History* (New York 3: Longmans Green & Co., 1913).

———, *The Life and Growth of Israel* (Toronto 5: General Board of Religious Education, The Church of England in Canada, 1931).

———, *The Tell el-Amarna Tablets* (New York 11: The Macmillan Co., 1939).

Meyer, E., *Geschichte des Altertums* (Stuttgart: J. G. Cottasche Buchhandlung, 1953-58).

Miller, M. S., and Miller, J. L., *Encyclopedia of Bible Life* (New York 16: Harper & Brothers, 1944).

Montgomery, J. A., *Arabia and the Bible* (Philadelphia 4: University of Pennsylvania Press, 1934).

Moscati, S., *Ancient Semitic Civilizations* (London, E.C. 1: Elek Books, 1957).

Mould, E. W. K., *Essentials of Bible History* (New York 17: The Ronald Press, 1951).

Neher, Andre and Renee, *Histoire Biblique du Peuple D'Israel* (Paris: Adrien-Maisonneuve, 1962).

North, C. R., *The Old Testament Interpretation of History* (London, E.C. 1: Epworth Press, 1946).

Noth, Martin, *The History of Israel* (New York 16: Harper & Brothers, 1958).

O'Callaghan, R. T., *Aram Naharaim* (Rome: Pontifical Biblical Institute, 1948).

Oesterley, W. O. E., *The Wisdom of Egypt and the Old Testament* (New York 11: The Macmillan Co., 1927).

Oesterley, W. O. E., and Robinson, T., *A History of Israel* (Oxford: Clarendon Press, 1932).

Olmstead, A. T., *History of Assyria* (New York 17: Charles Scribner's Sons, 1923).

———, *History of Palestine and Syria to the Persian Conquest* (New York 17: Charles Scribner's Sons, 1931).

———, *History of the Persian Empire* (Chicago 37: University of Chicago Press, 1948).

Orlinsky, Harry, *Ancient Israel* (Ithaca, N. Y.: Cornell University Press, 1954).

Payne, J. B., *An Outline of Hebrew History* (Grand Rapids 6: Baker Book House, 1954).

Peake, A. S., ed., *The People and the Book* (Oxford: Clarendon Press, 1940).

Pedersen, J., *Israel* (Copenhagen: Povl Branner, 1940).

Peet, T. E., *A Comparative Study of the Literatures of Egypt, Palestine, and Mesopotamia* (London, E.C. 4: Oxford University Press, 1931).

———, *Egypt and the Old Testament* (Liverpool 3: University Press of Liverpool, 1922).

Peritz, I. J., *Old Testament History* (Nashville 2: Abingdon Press, 1915).

Perkins, A. L., *The Comparative Archaeology of Early Mesopotamia* (Chicago 37: University of Chicago Press, 1949).

Pfeiffer, C. F., *Baker's Bible Atlas* (Grand Rapids: Baker Book House, 1961).

———, *The Patriarchal Age* (Grand Rapids: Baker Book House, 1961).

———, *Exile and Return* (Grand Rapids: Baker Book House, 1962).

Phillips, W., *Qataban and Sheba* (New York 17: Harcourt, Brace & Co., 1955).

Pieters, A., *Notes on Old Testament History* (Grand Rapids 3: William B. Eerdmans Publishing Co., 1950).

Price, I. M., *The Dramatic Story of Old Testament History* (Westwood, N. J.: Fleming H. Revell Co., 1935).

Price, I. M., Sellers, O. R., and Carlson, E. L., *The Monuments and the Old Testament* (Philadelphia 3: Judson Press, 1958).

Pritchard, J. B., *Ancient Near Eastern Texts* (Princeton, N. J.: Princeton University Press, 1950).

————, *The Ancient Near East in Pictures* (Princeton: Princeton University Press, 1954).

————, *Archaeology and the Old Testament* (Princeton: Princeton University Press, 1958).

Rawlinson, G., *History of Phoenicia* (New York 3: Longmans Green & Co., 1889).

Riciotti, G., *The History of Israel* (Milwaukee: Brace Publishing Co., 1955).

Robinson, G. L., *The Bearing of Archaeology on the Old Testament* (New York 19: American Tract Society, 1941).

————, *The Sarcophagus of an Ancient Civilization* (New York 11: The Macmillan Co., 1930).

Robinson, H. Wheeler, *The History of Israel* (London, W.C. 2: Duckworth, 1938).

Rogers, R. W., *Cuneiform Parallels to the Old Testament* (Nashville 2, Tenn.: Abingdon Press, 1926).

————, *History of Ancient Persia* (New York 17: Charles Scribner's Sons, 1929).

————, *A History of Babylonia and Assyria* (New York: Eaton & Mains, 1915 [now Abingdon Press, Nashville 2]).

Rowley, H. H., *From Joseph to Joshua* (London, E.C. 4: Oxford University Press, 1950).

————, *Recent Discovery and the Patriarchal Age* (Manchester 15, England: Manchester University Press, 1949).

————, *The Rediscovery of the Old Testament* (Philadelphia 7: Westminster Press, 1946).

Schultz, Samuel J., *The Old Testament Speaks* (New York: Harper & Brothers, 1960).

Schwartz, Leo, ed., *Great Ages and Ideas of the Jewish People* (New York 22: Random House, 1956).

Smith, G. A., *The Historical Geography of the Holy Land* (London, E.C. 4: Hodder & Stoughton, 1931).

Smith, Sidney, *Early History of Assyria to 1000 B.C.* (London, W.C. 2: Chatto & Windus, 1928).

Snaith, Norman, *The Jews from Cyrus to Herod* (Nashville 2: Abingdon Press, n.d.).

Steindorff, G., and Seele, K. C., *When Egypt Ruled the East* (Chicago 37: University of Chicago Press, 2nd ed., 1957).

Thiele, E. R., *The Mysterious Numbers of the Hebrew Kings* (Chicago 37: University of Chicago Press, 1951).

Thomas, D. W., ed., *Documents from Old Testament Times* (London, W.C. 2: Thomas Nelson & Sons, 1958).

Thompson, J. A., *Archaeology and the Old Testament* (Grand Rapids 3: William B. Eerdmans Publishing Co., 1957).

Unger, M. F., *Archaeology and the Old Testament* (Grand Rapids 6: Zondervan Publishing House, 1954).

————, *Israel and the Aramaeans of Damascus* (London, E.C. 4: James Clarke & Co., 1957).

Van der Meer, P., *The Ancient Chronology of Western Asia and Egypt* (Leiden, Netherlands: E. J. Brill, 1955).

White, J. A. M., *Ancient Egypt* (New York 16: Thomas Y. Crowell Co., 1953).

Whitley, C. F., *The Exilic Age* (Philadelphia 7: Westminster Press, 1957).

Wilson, J. A., *The Burden of Egypt* (Chicago 37: University of Chicago Press, 1951).

Wiseman, D. J., *Illustrations from Biblical Archaeology* (Grand Rapids 3: William B. Eerdmans Publishing Co., 1959).

Woolley, C. L., *Digging Up the Past* (London, E.C. 4: Ernest Benn, Ltd., 1930).

————, *The Sumerians* (London, E.C. 4: Clarendon Press, 1929).

————, *Ur of the Chaldees* (Harmondsworth, Middlesex, England: Penguin Books, 1950).

Wright, G. E., *Biblical Archaeology* (London: Gerald Duckworth & Co., 2nd ed., 1962).

————, *The Old Testament Against its Environment* (London, W.C. 1: S. C. M. Press, 1950).

Wright, G. E., and Filson, F. V., *The Westminster Historical Atlas to the Bible* (Philadelphia 7: Westminster Press, 1956).

In addition to the above books, the student should consult the following periodicals: "The Biblical Archaeologist," "Bulletin of the American Schools of Oriental Research," "Vetus Testamentum," "Orientalia," "Journal of Semitic Studies," "Journal of the American Oriental Society," "Journal of the Society of Biblical Literature."

INDEX